JUSTINE HENIN

FROM TRAGEDY TO TRIUMPH

MARK RYAN

BOOKS

First published in Great Britain in 2008 by
JR Books, 10 Greenland Street,
London NW1 0ND

Pictures in plate section:
Page 5 © Corbis
Pages 6, 7 and 8 © Rex features

A catalogue record for this book is available from the British Library.

ISBN 978-1-906217-45-7

1 3 5 7 9 10 8 6 4 2

Printed by MPG Books, Bodmin, Cornwall

CONTENTS

For my son, Luca, who was cheering for 'JuJu'
before he was three.

ACKNOWLEDGEMENTS

MY THANKS GO TO JEREMY ROBSON OF JR BOOKS, WHO must be Justine Henin's number one fan in the publishing world. Without Jeremy this project would never have got off the ground, and he has always been there when his help has been needed. His perceptive advice, born of a wisdom developed over many decades in the business, was simply invaluable from start to finish. He is a true gentleman and a pleasure to work with. For any writer it is always a great help to know that 'the boss' is every bit as passionate about a subject as you are. Together I hope we have struck the right balance between the emotive and objective, so that the reader can gain a genuine feel for Justine's unique story and what it means in a personal and sporting context.

I would also like to thank Lesley Wilson, Senior Editor at JR Books, who must be one of the most patient and professional people in the publishing game, and spent hours on the phone helping to make the book more readable.

At my end it would be unfair to overlook the efforts of my wife Victoria, who always came to the rescue of her technophobe husband when computer literacy was urgently required to solve all manner of problems.

In the world of journalism my thanks go to all those skilled and hard-working scribes whose interviews have helped to build up the picture painted here, while in the tennis world I would like to pay tribute to the amazing WTA tour, and the female gladiators whose exploits on court continue to make the Grand Slam venues the most exciting and dramatic stages in sport.

Finally the inside story of Justine's moving family history, and her troubled journey to maturity, could never have been told without the openness and honesty shown by so many of her relatives down the years, led by her irrepressible father, Jose. Each member of the Henin family is truly unique and lovable, and I salute you all for your humour and resilience. It has been an honour to be allowed into your lives for long enough to piece together the narrative offered here. I hope you all consider the end result to be a fitting monument to your strength and your capacity to enjoy life, despite some of the very painful episodes you have had to endure.

CHAPTER 1
THE TEST

WHEN SHE KNEW HER MARRIAGE WAS DEAD, SELF-DOUBT took hold. One minute a confident Justine Henin could bask in the glory of being the toughest and the best, the next she had entered a nightmare so personally devastating that she wondered whether she would cope at all.

Maybe the latest crisis shouldn't have come as quite such a shock to Henin, who had learned early just how beautiful and cruel life could be. She had lost her mother before she was even a teenager, and yet she had bounced back to tame the giants of the game and climb to the top of the sporting world. In reaching such heights it appeared that she had left behind her own vulnerability.

Yet Justine's split from her husband, Pierre-Yves Hardenne, left her in a state of such turmoil at the start of 2007 that she pulled out of the Australian Open, one of only four Grand Slam events in the tennis calendar. For the number one player in the world, who needed to stay in the fight to keep her rivals at bay, such a public retreat spelt potential disaster. But this wasn't just about sport any more.

Hardenne, a skinny, high-cheeked young man who often appeared aloof and moody, had captured Justine's heart some eight years earlier, and had remained central to almost everything she had done since. As a troubled young woman, she had shunned her surviving family to be with the husband from whom she was now breaking away. No wonder the separation signalled the start of a confused, frightening time for Justine, and she knew she would need all her legendary courage just to stay afloat . . .

The tennis world looked on. It seemed the complete player had an Achilles heel after all. The legendary Martina Navratilova had called her 'the female Federer'; she was the sensation whose backhand John McEnroe had described as 'the finest shot in the game – women's or men's'. But it was her inner steel that usually gave her the edge over her opponents; and now she seemed frail.

Justine's unmatchable passion and fighting spirit had always made up for her lack of height and weight. Billie Jean King, whose own fearsome approach had blazed the trail for the modern women's game, had once hailed her as 'pound for pound the best women's athlete I have ever seen'. Now Justine, who was less than five feet six inches tall and weighed in at just 126 pounds, seemed very vulnerable indeed. In public, at least, she tried to put on a brave face. 'I will return to you', she assured her fans, and they waited anxiously for more news.

Her supporters and those around her worried for Justine, and questioned whether she would be in a fit emotional state to defend her French title in May. Perhaps she would choose instead to take an indefinite break from the game, while she learned to cope with the grim prospect of divorce.

She sat down and grieved for her marriage as her rivals played the Australian Open without her. 'I didn't know if I was going to be able to overcome these problems,' she said later.

Justine faced her situation bravely. One great love of her life was gone, and there was no going back; but another remained, waiting patiently for her, and that other love was tennis. It had claimed a special place in her heart long before Pierre-Yves, and it was still there now, along with her coach and guru, Carlos Rodriguez. 'It was important to keep working, to keep busy, so tennis was like therapy,' she explained later.

Justine returned in February and played a tournament in Paris. She didn't win it, but soon she was playing with all her old determination. By March she was well on the way to a full recovery. Then, just when all seemed well, another powerful blow threw her off balance. While in Barcelona for the Laureus Sports Awards, she received a text from her sister, Sarah, warning that David Henin, her plump and sensitive elder brother, had been seriously injured in a car crash and was lying in a coma.

It had been seven years since Justine had enjoyed a normal, loving relationship with David; seven years since she had hugged her other brother, Thomas; seven years since she had publicly acknowledged her father, Jose. The dying wish of her mother, Francoise, had been that the family stayed together. But Justine believed that her own identity was at stake and felt unable to put her family first.

The last time David had spoken publicly about his estrangement from Justine had been prior to her Australian Open campaign of 2004. Then he had said: 'It's a shame that my sister is so heavily influenced by those around her.

But we who have not been afforded the slightest contact for the last few years will continue to get up in the middle of the night to support her.'

A number of factors had contributed to Justine's decision to leave her family behind, stunned and embittered; but seven years later, with David at death's door, was anyone's grievance still powerful enough to warrant a continuation of the feud? That is what she had to weigh up when her sister Sarah broke the news about the accident. To drop everything and run to David's hospital bedside wasn't necessarily as straightforward as it seemed. Perhaps, during such a stressful time, some of her relatives might resent her presence. Maybe it would be better to wait. But to do that was equally risky, with David's life hanging in the balance.

Nothing enhances love like the fear that someone might be about to die. It was the sort of moment that must have made the Henin family wonder how on earth they had allowed their feud to continue for so long, and how they had come to draw such destructive battle lines between themselves in the first place.

CHAPTER 2

PIERRE-YVES AND THE DANCE

IN AUGUST 1998, A 16-YEAR-OLD JUSTINE HENIN WAS DUE to present the prize at an amateur tournament in her family's home village of Han-sur-Lesse. This Belgian backwater was famous for its spectacular caves, a hidden world beneath the gentle wooded hills that formed the gateway to the Ardennes. The tennis club was tucked away discreetly, a sideshow to the main tourist attraction. Jose Henin, larger than life in more ways than one, had officiated at the club in times gone by, and it was only natural that his daughter, a rising star in the tennis world, should be asked to present the trophy to the tournament winner. Word had it that Justine Henin might soon be as famous as the caves themselves, if only she could translate her stunning form from the junior to the senior circuit.

Pierre-Yves Hardenne, a local lad and a relative newcomer to the game, entered the Han-sur-Lesse competition for fun. It was the first time he had ever played in such a tournament. Amazingly, he won it. When Justine stepped up to congratulate the victor, who was more than a year older than she was, something about his broad, boyish smile caused her to return it with interest. Sparks flew as their eyes met and they both felt a pure joy, something akin to love at first sight.

The impact of that seismic moment would be felt by many others over time, and life would change for Justine and Pierre-Yves who, as their relationship developed into marriage, would take on the strength of the other. For a good number of years anyone who tried to get in their way would be given reason to wish they had not done so. Among those they left reeling in their wake were many members of Justine's own family, whom she blamed for not making Pierre-Yves feel more welcome. She would claim later: 'It was not Pierre-Yves my family didn't like. It was the thought of there being anyone in my life. But when I met Pierre-Yves, I thought, "At last, you can be happy."'

Happiness had seemed elusive since Justine's mother, Francoise, had died when the tennis-crazy child was just 12 years old. An increased sense of responsibility at home appeared to clash with Henin's sporting ambitions. In an interview in 2003, Justine explained: 'After my mother died it was never the same. It is wrong to say I became the mother of the family, because I didn't cook or anything like that. But I was mature very early and they all used to come to me with their problems, my two older brothers and my young sister. It became difficult. I lead a special life – I have to. But they didn't understand and then there were money problems and jealousy. It was impossible.'

Her family didn't agree with that analysis of the

domestic dynamic. At the height of their feud, her father, Jose, hit back: 'Everything in the family was geared to Justine's success and the others suffered as a result. They don't complain now, only Justine. I don't try to claim I was a perfect father. I was depressed and put on weight, around twenty kilos. But I did my best when faced with difficult circumstances, and the other children understood what was happening to me. And through this, I always put Justine's career first. Everyone knows that.'

Her feisty brother Thomas was equally incensed by the attack: 'We were not jealous of Pierre-Yves and I didn't have any big showdown with Justine over it. For her to say that we didn't accept him, or came to her with our problems, just makes it easier for her to excuse her departure. She was young and we all had problems, the children and my father included.'

However, back in 2001, Justine's coach, Carlos Rodriguez, with whom most people credit Henin's climb to the summit of women's tennis, described Jose's and the family's attitude to his daughter like this: 'I don't know how to say it in English but he, the father, tried to appropriate her. They did not respect her needs. I saw what they were doing to her and I spoke up very quickly. We had many arguments, her father and I.'

The stakes were high in late 1998. Justine was about to turn professional, and already she looked capable of breaking into the elite group at the top end of the senior rankings. For years, most of the family income had been directed towards taking her where she wanted to be. The big sporting management agency International Management Group (IMG) had been on the scene for some time, taking care of many aspects of Justine's career. But Jose had escorted his daughter to tournaments, while his brother, Jean-Paul, had helped to finance her early career. Jose explained: 'It took a lot of money to finance Justine's tennis development over all those years. When we travelled we used to take just one bedroom, to save money. I used to pay half the bill, so it was actually cheaper for the Belgian Federation [who sponsored Justine] when I was there. Every month we paid a contribution for Carlos, and one for me to travel. We paid for the car and I personally drove about a thousand miles a week, taking Justine to tournaments or wherever else she needed to be. Then there was some tax to pay on the earnings as well, of course.'

As she began to earn good money, Jose thought it only fair that some of that outlay should be repaid to those within the family who had financed her tennis development in the first place or made sacrifices to help set her on the road to stardom; he also thought that his other children should benefit too, not least the 12-year-old Sarah, who had behaved so graciously as Justine's lifestyle on the junior circuit demanded the lion's share of her father's attention during her formative years. As far as her father was concerned, this wasn't 'appropriation' – how could it be when Justine was his daughter? – but simply the restoration of balance.

The arrival of Pierre-Yves on the scene, and the start of what seemed like a typical teenage love affair, threatened to put that process in doubt. Even so, Jose denied Justine's claim that her family didn't want Pierre-Yves or any other potential boyfriend in her life, insisting that it was quite the reverse, and that Pierre-Yves was in his house all the time.

The romance lasted through winter into spring, and Justine's performance on court showed no signs of suffering. By early summer and the 1999 French Open it seemed that, far from being a hindrance to Justine's career, Pierre-Yves might just prove to be an inspiration. Having gained entry as a qualifier, Henin won through her opener to face the highly ranked American Lindsay Davenport in the second round. No one gave Justine, not yet 17, the slightest chance against an established powerhouse such as Davenport, especially when she lost the first set 6-3. But when Justine hit back to take the second set 6-2, a watching John McEnroe could scarcely believe his eyes. 'It was incredible how she hit the ball,' he recalled later.

Henin wasn't done, even serving for the match at 5-4 in the third, but Davenport used her superior experience to show the coolest composure when it mattered, and eventually scraped through 7-5. While Justine was kicking herself, McEnroe knew he had seen something special. 'Few people are born with such potential,' he said simply. Before long, he had become Henin's number one celebrity fan, declaring: 'She is the player I most like to watch.'

Justine's fantastic showing prompted a double celebration when she got home, since 1 June was also her 17th birthday. At a party in a restaurant near the Han-sur-Lesse tennis club, Thomas and Justine danced uninhibitedly; and Pierre-Yves seemed to take exception. Thomas, who was slender and handsome in his twenties, recalled later: 'I was dancing with Justine that night and my girlfriend, Vanessa, was having a cigarette, off to the side. Pierre-Yves went up to her and pointed to us dancing. He asked her what she thought about it. She didn't know what he was talking about. But Pierre-Yves said that Justine was too close to me, and that the situation couldn't continue, he didn't like it. That's when our problems began.'

Had Pierre-Yves walked into Justine's life in 1996, 1997 or even in the first quarter of 1998, he might have had a reason to resent the strength of the bond between brother and sister. At that time Thomas had unselfishly put his own plans on hold to help make his sister's dreams come true. He had delayed his studies, so essential to his preferred career in banking, in order to live alongside Justine at a tennis academy, the Centre of Excellence in Mons, run by the Belgian Tennis Federation (or more precisely its French-speaking branch, the Association Francophone de Tennis). Thomas worked with all the children, but primarily he was there to make life easier for Justine, who was the only girl among all the hopefuls.

Then in April 1998 Thomas met Vanessa, and fell in love. As the months went by, he felt it was time to start thinking again of his own career. He said: 'I wanted my life back. I had been working with Justine and we were very close. But I told her in December 1998 that I wanted to work for myself now, that I could not go on escorting her on the professional circuit. She was very upset, but my position was this: life with her wasn't a job for me. I wanted to work in a bank and I did so. My life now was with Vanessa.'

So by the time of the party after the French Open in the early summer of 1999, a spontaneous dance between a brother and sister who still loved each other dearly shouldn't have given Justine's boyfriend cause for concern. Yet it obviously did and when Pierre-Yves sought to question Justine's relationship with Thomas, Jose naturally supported his son, as did Thomas's brother, David.

However, to Justine it looked as though Jose had made a clear choice in favour of his other children, against her.

Jose revealed: 'Later Justine came and said "That was a big mistake, to choose David and Thomas instead of me and Pierre-Yves."' Jose would pay dearly for the stand he had made, on a number of levels.

It may have been Thomas who first clashed with Pierre-Yves but Jose wasn't very far behind. As he recalled: 'We were eating dinner one night and I told him that I thought it was important for him to think about a career for himself, and work out what he wanted to do in life. I said he should be his own man. He didn't like being given that advice one bit, and it was just the start of the tension between us. Yes, I was also annoyed that Justine wasn't giving much time to the family any more. And I may have feared that Pierre-Yves's increasing influence was going to undermine Justine's professionalism towards her tennis; but I was thinking of him too, when I said those things.'

Like many teenagers, Pierre-Yves refused to be told how to live his life. And Jose admitted that had he been in Pierre-Yves's shoes he might have reacted in exactly the same way. One of Jose's brothers, Jean-Marie, wasn't so understanding when his greeting to Pierre-Yves was thrown back in his face at around the same time.

It seems that there were several members of the Henin family Pierre-Yves didn't respect and by coincidence Justine seemed to be showing her relations less respect by the day, too. By the time they all came together for another dinner, towards the end of 1999, Pierre-Yves apparently felt so confident of his relationship with Justine that, according to Jose, he came right out and told her: 'I think it would be better if you lived away from your family home so that you are self-sufficient.'

In 2007, Justine disputed this version of events, and said: 'Pierre-Yves wasn't so close to my family, but he never told me to leave them.'

Perhaps he didn't need to.

CHAPTER 3
BRUTAL DIAMOND

CARLOS RODRIGUEZ DIDN'T TRY TO TELL JUSTINE THAT Pierre-Yves was bad for her tennis career, quite the reverse. Justine's swarthy coach quietly supported her, as she gradually became opposed to her father's influence on any aspect of her life. The irony, given the way the two men soon found themselves on opposite sides in the family split, was that it had been Jose who had insisted upon Rodriguez being Justine's coach several years earlier.

The Argentinian had leapt to prominence at Wimbledon in the mid-1990s, helping the lower-ranked Dick Norman beat Stefan Edberg. In 1996 he had been working for the Association Francophone de Tennis (AFT), the French-speaking arm of the Belgian Tennis Federation, and his growing reputation had caught Jose's eye. When Justine's father met the charismatic South American in person, it only served to confirm his positive impressions. 'I gave Justine to Carlos – he was my choice,' Jose explained. 'We had some conversations and I enjoyed his views on tennis. I liked his ideas for training and practice. He was interesting.'

Therefore Jose called the AFT's technical director, Eduardo Masso, with a proposal. Justine would work under the federation at the Centre of Excellence in Mons, as long as Carlos Rodriguez would help coach her.

For the Argentinian, it wasn't difficult to agree to the arrangement once he had met Justine. Although the physical specimen placed before him was less than impressive, her tennis looked promising enough. But that wasn't what got Carlos so excited initially. 'In her eyes, from the first time I saw her, there was this flame,' said Rodriguez revealingly. 'She was a brutal diamond, like nothing else Belgian tennis had ever seen. More than her talent to start with, it was her attitude, this desire always to do the best she could, this incredibly professional way of doing things, that made me want to work with her.'

His impact on her game was almost immediate. Together Justine, Rodriguez and Jose travelled to the Orange Bowl in Miami, effectively the world under-14s tennis championships. Incredibly, Justine won the tournament.

By now a spotty, tomboyish teenager, the delighted young champion sent a photograph of herself to her aunt and uncle soon afterwards, on which she wrote: 'Aunt Clelia and Uncle Jean-Paul, I offer you this photo, taken just after the Orange Bowl, as a little souvenir of my victory. I won't write an essay, I just want to thank you for everything that you do for me. I know that I can count on you, and that you will always be there for me. I'm very lucky to have uncles and aunts like you. Thanks for everything, Big Kisses, Justine.' At the height of the family feud, when they too were sidelined, it was a note they would re-read ruefully.

Strongly supported by the family and inspired by her new coach Rodriguez, Henin went from strength to strength in 1996 and 1997. She won the European under-14s title in San Remo, Italy, to confirm her class. She also represented Belgium at under-14s level, often sharing hotel rooms with future rival Kim Clijsters, who came from the Flemish part of Belgium.

In the early summer of 1997 Justine began her assault on Junior Roland Garros, although she encountered problems in the semi-final against Nathalie Dechy. Having already lost the first set 5-7, Henin faced four match points in the second, but somehow survived each time with audacious shots which just managed to clip the line. That sort of defiance was too much for Dechy, who eventually crumbled. Justine came through 5-7, 7-6, 6-1, and suddenly she was one step away from French Junior Open glory.

Her paternal grandparents, Alphonse and Jeanne, had travelled to the tournament and watched as she faced Cara Black in the final, losing the first set 4-6. Typically, she hit back to take the next two sets, 6-4, 6-4, and was crowned champion. Victory signified more than just a title to Justine: 'When I won the French Open Juniors, I knew it was going to be my job.'

At the age of 15 she claimed the Belgian national title, beating a top-40 ranked player called Dominique Van Roost in the process. But 1997 wasn't all plain sailing, and ominously Jose's relationship with Carlos and the Belgian Tennis Federation became strained. Jose argued that the physical problems Justine often encountered were being mishandled. He recalled: 'She had a foot injury in 1997, which lingered for weeks. The doctor diagnosed tendonitis, so she was given cortisone injections for the inflammation. But in fact the foot was broken; and you can't use cortisone in such a case, because there is a risk of decalcification.'

When the federation finally realised their mistake, they sent Justine to Brussels where she was given a leg support to walk with, but by then two months had already passed. Eventually Jose's friend Eddie Merckx, the famous cyclist and Tour de France winner, sent her to a specialist he knew. After three months' work with a physiotherapist, she was finally fit again.

The next year, however, Justine developed digestive problems just as she was about to make her first appearance for Belgium in Bratislava, in the Federation Cup. Jose asked a doctor about the problem and was told she could go on the trip, even though she looked pale and drawn. But the doctor warned that if she needed a hospital out there, then the military hospitals were the best option – hardly reassuring.

Justine left on the Monday and Jose joined her out there on the Thursday, as part of the federation officials and supporters' trip. She was very tired, and medical tests before she returned home revealed the presence of harmful microbes in her intestines. She went home that Saturday, but had to have three months lay-off as she recovered from a course of antibiotics. 'I wasn't the only one to voice the opinion that it was a mistake that she had been cleared for the trip in the first place' Jose explained. 'The federation should have known something was wrong and she shouldn't have gone. It wasn't good for her and it wasn't good for the team; if I was getting nervous, it was because she was always injured or sick. I began to think that maybe she wasn't right for the sport after all. I lost confidence in the doctors, in the federation and in Carlos Rodriguez.'

But the more Jose complained, the more he played into the hands of the professionals who wanted to take control

of Justine's career. Perhaps he was also giving them ammu-
nition to brand him as a typically pushy tennis parent, for
when Justine was fit again and a newly turned professional
in 1999, Jose was the one trying to insist that she should
use the wild-card entries that IMG-connected players
could sometimes gain to the notable tournaments.
Rodriguez, for his part, appeared to favour a more gradual
progression for Justine under his own close supervision.
Tensions began to build beneath the surface as Jose and
Carlos – with Justine stuck in the middle – toured the
world with increasingly differing views about the direction
she should be taking.

On a particularly shocking occasion, however, such
concerns were put to one side. They had gone to play a
USTA (United States Tennis Association) challenger
tournament about 25 or 30 miles outside Chicago in
Rockford, Illinois. The total prize money on offer was
$25,000. They had talked a lot about this trip beforehand,
laughing about the city's violent reputation, with its
gangster history. Jose recalled: 'When we came out of
Chicago's O'Hare International airport, Carlos, Justine
and I were all feeling pretty relaxed, until – the first thing
we saw was a dead body. A policeman had just shot this
black man. I don't know why. But he was lying there, face
down in a pool of blood, stone dead. The officer who had
killed him still had his gun out of the holster and various
cops were moving around the body. Justine stayed pretty
quiet, but then she reacted to most situations like that, and
I think of the three of us Carlos was the most shocked.'

They got away as quickly as possible, trying to put what
they had seen behind them. After all, Justine had a
tournament to play and she did well enough, reaching the

quarter-finals. But the three of them remembered the incident outside the airport more than anything and couldn't help talking about it for days afterwards.

There were plenty of other tournaments more notable for Justine's performance on the court in 1999. Selected for Belgium's Federation Cup team, she won both of her matches to help her country defeat Holland 3-2. She also became only the fifth player to win a debut WTA (Women's Tennis Association) Tour title when, having gained a wild-card entry to the Antwerp Tournament, she surprised everyone by beating Sarah Pitkowski, who had a world ranking of 35, in the final. Henin's 6-1, 6-2 demolition of such a respected opponent gave a tantalising taste of what was to come.

And so it came to the French Open, the big fight against Lindsay Davenport, the party afterwards, and Justine's dance with her brother Thomas. By the end of that night, Pierre-Yves was on a collision course with the Henin family.

Carlos Rodriguez must have realised that he was soon going to have to choose a side when the family war broke out, and since he felt that Jose Henin treated his daughter too much like a commodity, and could see her just itching to break away, it was probably inevitable that he began to develop a rapport with Hardenne – especially since, unlike Jose, Pierre-Yves never challenged his authority on tennis matters. As allies, they knew they could give Justine all the support she required at the time.

Her coach's acceptance of Pierre-Yves meant everything to Justine. She felt understood on every level by the two men she regarded as most important to her future. To Carlos Rodriguez, the idea that Justine might leave home so young wouldn't have seemed so strange. He had done precisely the same back in Argentina aged 17, so he would have seen little reason to discourage such ambitions in his protégée.

Justine mulled over her options that summer putting everything on hold to take a shot at the US Open in September, against her father's advice. However, the sort of impact she had made against Davenport in Paris was not to be repeated so soon. She was drawn against the powerfully built Amelie Mauresmo and found herself knocked out in the first round. Jose claimed later: 'After that I told Justine that I felt it was time to create some distance between us. I was nervous, I didn't even think it had been a good idea for her to play that tournament. I told her that Sarah needed me. She was only 13.'

A once-loving relationship between father and daughter was in serious danger of being torn asunder.

CHAPTER 4
TIE-BREAK

ALTHOUGH JUSTINE WASN'T QUITE READY TO MAKE THE final professional break from her father, towards the end of 1999 she did go to play a big tournament without him – the Advanta Championships in Philadelphia. This was no small test for Justine, not after what she had been through in Chicago earlier in the year. She passed with flying colours and claimed her first big scalp, a glamorous one at that. Anna Kournikova was a top-10 player and big news at the time; but Justine attacked the net, fed off Kournikova's nerves, and proved she was better than at least one of the so-called superstars of the sport. She won a tie-break to take the first set, closed out the second 6-4, and could hardly contain her delight.

'She phoned to tell me what she'd done,' said Jose, explaining what it had meant to her. 'I was so happy. I said, "That's great! You see! You can do it without me. Go it alone from here." She said, "I prefer it when you are there with me."'

Jose remembered the moment with pride, not just because it was one of Justine's first great victories on the professional circuit, but because he believed it proved that he was not always trying to play the pushy father. He felt he was merely a man who made mistakes, like any other parent, and tried to put them right as he went along. As he explained later: 'I'm not stupid, I know that it isn't always good for a player to have their father watching over their shoulder while they are on court. I pushed her too hard sometimes, but I was the first to see that. We needed some distance because effectively we had been on the tennis circuit together for 10 years already.'

For Jose, his relationship with his daughter was never the black-and-white story of hero and villain often portrayed in the media. And the call from Philadelphia suggested that, despite frayed nerves on both sides, the child in Justine was also reluctant to cut ties with her father. In reality, however, the process had already begun, and her inner conflict wouldn't last long.

It soon dawned on Jose that what he said didn't seem to matter any more, either in his daughter's tennis life or her personal life. He later recalled: 'Justine and I had a big fight before we left for Australia at the start of 2000. I was reluctant to accompany her.' By the time they reached the Australian Open, relations had sunk to an all-time low. According to Jose, Justine's heart didn't seem to be in her tennis. She was always calling Pierre-Yves back in Belgium, whether it was seven in the morning or eleven at night. The time difference obviously didn't help her sleeping pattern. To Jose it was as if she was more interested in the phone calls. It was no surprise to him when she was knocked out early. Martina Hingis was her second-round executioner, winning 6-3, 6-3.

It was only a matter of time before the tension in their already-strained relationship boiled over into something more decisive. In February 2000, Justine was due to play in the Open Gaz, an important indoor tournament in Paris. On the day of the short journey to the French capital from Belgium, her maternal grandfather, Georges Rosiere, came to see her off. As Justine's number one fan, he too had felt the impact of her affair with Pierre-Yves.

Georges had already complained to Jose on six or seven separate occasions that he didn't see Justine any more. Now he had come to give her a warm send-off and she simply wasn't there at the appointed time. Since Georges was becoming agitated, Jose thought he'd better do something about it. They both knew where she would be – round at her boyfriend's house. In the end, Jose went to fetch her and found her sitting on Pierre-Yves' lap as if she had forgotten her responsibilities to the rest of her family.

'When I told her she was late and that her grandfather was waiting to say goodbye, she finally tore herself away from Pierre-Yves and came back with me,' explained Jose. 'We got there and I told her how selfish and unprofessional I thought she was becoming, because her kit wasn't even packed and ready. I also scolded her for keeping her grandfather waiting so long. What shocked me then was that Georges, whose agitated state had contributed to the tension, suddenly took Justine's side against me, I couldn't believe it. I had tried to make sure she did the right thing, in order to please him as well, and now I was suddenly the bad guy in everyone's eyes.'

Eventually, Justine and Jose got in the car and drove off to Paris. But Jose had made up his mind that this was going to be the last time he would escort her to a tournament. If Justine hadn't already come to the same conclusion, she soon would.

The tournament started well enough with her win over the better-known Magdalena Maleeva in the first round. Then she came up against the might of world number six Nathalie Tauziat, and lost the first set 5-7. What she produced next shocked many observers, who witnessed a ferocious comeback against a more fancied opponent. As Justine took that second set 6-2, she and everyone else watching knew that she had what it took to be massive in the sport. Yet somewhere inside Justine's head it suddenly all seemed to go wrong. The fire went out, Tauziat was back in control and the favourite claimed the last set 6-4. It was a match Justine felt she could have won.

In the car on the way back, Jose drove while Justine and Carlos Rodriguez sat quietly as passengers. Jose broke the silence and said: 'I don't understand why you played to Tauziat's strengths all the time.'

'What do you mean?' Justine asked.

'You kept playing to her backhand,' Jose insisted.

'Well I'm not sure I should have played to her forehand all the time,' Justine argued.

Carlos cut in to support his player. 'I'm not sure she should have played to Tauziat's forehand either.'

And in that moment Jose felt he was on the outside, looking in on Justine's career, outvoted, undermined, and given the firm impression that his opinion no longer counted for very much at all. The growing tensions between father and daughter resulted in numerous arguments, and in March it reached the point where Justine told her father she was going to stay with her aunt, Genevieve, at least until the air had been cleared. Her aunt, who lived just around the corner, agreed that it might be the best thing for all concerned, but Jose wasn't having it.

Later he remembered that day with sadness. 'I said something terrible to Justine, something I should never have said and would always regret. I looked her in the eye and told her, "If you walk out of that door, you will not be my daughter any more." She walked out of the door.'

CHAPTER 5

THE AFTERMATH

JUSTINE WAS ANGRY AND UPSET. AT FIRST HER AUNT Genevieve tried to help her to look at the situation more calmly, as they were living under the same roof for the time being, but her efforts were in vain. Justine wasn't feeling objective or forgiving, and any hope of a family crisis being averted through compromise quickly disappeared. As far as Justine was concerned she had been wronged. Pretty soon 'things got out of proportion', as Justine put it later. With hindsight, looking back at her 'miscommunication with my father and brothers', she admitted that 'when you're 17 or 18 years old you don't know a lot of things'. At the time, however, she thought she knew enough to condemn Jose, Thomas and David outright, because in her eyes 'they would not accept my boyfriend', and because 'my father was too involved in my tennis career. Everyone was taking the decisions that should have been mine'.

She regarded this 'impossible' attitude as an assault on everything she held dear, including, perhaps, even her very identity. Typically, she came out fighting, and her reaction was extreme. From the moment she left home, her attitude to her family was black and white: you were either with her in each decision she took, or else you were against her.

Thomas and David were cast aside. They had made it clear that they didn't appreciate Pierre-Yves' attitude to the Henin family. To Justine that appeared to be a declaration of war; and the leader of the enemy was Jose. Her father's threat to disown her must have been the last straw. The notion that Jose had lashed out in the heat of the moment, and could never have meant what he had said, escaped her. As he remarked later: 'What I said was not good, but it shouldn't have been a reason to break with the family as she did.'

Unfortunately, however, Jose's threat might have also sounded like a challenge to Justine, issued to see if she really had the guts to stand on her own two feet and defy the family at such a tender age. So instead of stepping back from the brink, to discuss together what had so hurt each wounded party, the Henin family marched headlong into their feud. Justine later admitted: 'OK, I didn't know I wouldn't see my family for seven years, but that's what happened because we were too proud, perhaps, or we weren't open enough at the time. There was wrong on both sides.'

That sort of measured perspective wasn't available to her as a fiery teenager, or indeed a young woman who quickly revelled in her newfound independence. Family history had told her that life could be tragically short, particularly if you were female. She seemed determined to go in search of romantic and professional highs unhindered by complications, fearing perhaps that the lows suffered by other women in her family might be just around the corner, waiting for her too. She seized the day, and she loved the thrill of liberation.

As soon as she had made the move to her aunt's house it seemed as though a weight had been lifted from her shoulders. Gone was a life in which she felt she had to be strong for everyone else, and play pressure-cooker tennis with her father breathing down her neck. 'Before I left, I was under a lot of pressure in terms of my tennis. After I left, I wasn't so afraid to lose,' she observed later. Now she would be strong for herself, pursue her tennis ambitions for her own reasons, and above all see Pierre-Yves when she wanted – which was pretty much whenever she wasn't playing tennis.

So March 2000 heralded a decisive new phase in Justine's life. The more she found that she could cope without her immediate family, the more she resented the way her life had been before. She wanted to lash out, and her parting shots were fired with a venom that set the tone for the new hostility. As Jose painfully recalled: 'She returned home to visit us a few times. During one of those visits, I asked her: "Why are you saying I'm a bad father? A few months ago you said I was a good father. You said publicly that you were lucky to have a father like me".' According to Jose, Justine turned to him and replied: 'I said that to please you – but I didn't think it.' He added later: 'It really broke my heart when she said that.'

Thomas believed that Justine was being unfair, and found her subsequent outbursts against their father distasteful. He said: 'It was her choice to leave and I respect that. But I do not respect the fact that she criticised my father. Sarah, David and I, we all know that our father did all he could for us. He was always a very good father.'

Home videos of family holidays to North America and everyday life around Han-sur-Lesse certainly seem to indicate a loving father and a happy child. If Justine hadn't been so very good at tennis, perhaps she would have had no cause for complaint. But all parents are keen for their child to fulfil their potential; and it is easy to go too far in trying to ensure that a God-given talent isn't squandered, especially one so close to a father's heart. Thomas and David were never going to back Justine and Pierre-Yves against Jose; they would remain loyal instead to the father who had brought them up the best way he could, for all his faults. The resentment hardened on both sides.

For Jose, the breakdown in family relations would prove costly, and not just emotionally. Carlos Rodriguez once alleged that it was Justine who felt the financial impact of her departure from the family home. He said: 'There was the money problem. When she left home at 17 she had nothing – not 10 Belgian francs. The Belgian federation had to pay everything for her.' Rodriguez painted a picture which seemed to suggest that Justine was virtually living on handouts from her aunts Francoise and Genevieve during this period, and indeed they did both play a big part in sustaining Justine's bid for independence. Jose accepts that she might have had no money in her pocket when she walked out of his door; but then she was only going to stay with her aunt, nearby. He insisted that money had been placed in accounts for her, in readiness for when she turned 18. She had a highly professional management organisation, IMG, looking after many of her interests, and it was unlikely that she would ever be left in need of cash. At that time she wasn't supposed to receive money anyway since she wasn't yet 18. Justine's handsome uncle Jean-Paul said:

'The feud hit Jose in the pocket a lot harder than it hit Justine. He was the one who was really hurt financially.'

Jean-Marie, Jose's tough-looking brother, told me: 'Jose was always a good sportsman when he was younger and maybe he started to live some of his sporting dreams through Justine, like she was his protégée as well as his daughter. But why does she say she had to separate from her family in order to succeed in her tennis career? That's crazy! The Williams' sisters had their father and mother around them, and they did pretty well! Justine was playing great tennis when she had her family around her too. She was the best in the world at various teenage levels, it didn't just suddenly happen.'

And the big breakthrough wasn't going to happen just yet either, though suddenly the future superstar felt she could move at her own pace. Pierre-Yves and Carlos began to give her a sense of control over her own destiny, and she loved them for it. In fact Justine was so happy with Pierre-Yves that she moved in with him. They took a simple flat above a butcher's shop in Marloie, near Han-sur-Lesse. It was quite a step for the young lovers to take, but how else could they maximise their precious time together, away from the pressures of the tour? Much as Justine adored her aunts, she was 18 now and she felt it was time to strike out on her own. Pierre-Yves decided to sacrifice his studies, so he could dedicate himself to supporting Justine on tour in any way he could. The alternative would have been to live apart for half of each year, and neither of them wanted that. They were falling more and more deeply for each other, and although Pierre-Yves risked compromising his own independence by building his life around Justine's, it was a risk he was prepared to take. For a good many years it even worked.

Understandably, 2000 was very much a transitional year for Justine Henin on the tennis court, as it was away from the game. She had executed great changes in all aspects of her life. But by the time that year came to an end, her head was clear and she was ready to play tennis like never before.

CHAPTER 6

ENGAGEMENT AND BEREAVEMENT

WITH JUSTINE AND PIERRE-YVES NOW LIVING TOGETHER, Jose's worst fears seemed to have been confirmed. He thought that any rival for Justine's attentions would destroy her focus on tennis, and one day leave her wishing that she had been more disciplined in maintaining her priorities. It was Jose, after all, who had taken her to the verge of great sporting success and there were financial implications to consider. What he couldn't see, and might not have wanted to contemplate in any detail, was that Pierre-Yves was making Justine ecstatically happy in a way he never could. Hardenne was an integral part of her new life, her new identity – her independence. And while that continued, he was likely to be good for her tennis too.

For two rounds of the 2001 Australian Open, Justine let her racket do the talking and notched up easy wins. Then she gave an extremely revealing press conference. She said: 'I am not so nervous as last year and I think I can play without problems in my head. I had injuries and I had personal problems last year, and now it is in the past and I can do my best on court . . . I am here with my coach and fiancé.' For those who didn't already know, the strength of her commitment to Pierre-Yves was no longer open to any doubt.

'When are you getting married?' she was asked by her stunned media audience.

'Married?' She said it almost as though she hadn't considered the obvious implication of the word 'fiancé'.

'Yes,' the interviewer replied simply.

Justine smiled and answered: 'I think in the next two years.'

Having broken the news, such was the nature of her life that she just went back to work in a carefree way, and won her next match at the Australian Open to set up a fourth-round showdown with Monica Seles.

As we shall see later, Seles and her fighting spirit held a very special place in Justine's childhood memories. And although the Monica who met Justine in Melbourne in 2001 wasn't quite such a formidable force, she was still seeded four for the tournament. So everyone was staggered when Henin came out with all guns blazing and took the first set 6-4. Before long, however, that chilling Seles yelp was back to its full, shrill capacity. Realising that she was in serious danger of being dumped out of the tournament by an underdog, she stepped up her game to take the final two sets 6-4 and with them the match. But Justine returned to Europe with her head held high, knowing that she had given the tennis world an indication of what she could achieve in the future.

Back home Justine didn't visit her father to tell him personally what she had told the rest of the world. She probably thought such a move would only invite pleas from him for her to reconsider, even that he would be angry at how the news had come out in the first place. So it was left to Jose to read the newspapers and comment equally publicly on the startling development. He said: 'Whatever problems we've had, my place is with my daughter on that day, leading her down the aisle. That's where I still hope to be.' Jose's message couldn't have been clearer. He wished to bury his differences with his daughter and Pierre-Yves, and accept Hardenne into his family, since marriage was by now inevitable anyway. Ominously, however, he received no reply, either privately or publicly.

Justine was concentrating on her tennis meanwhile, and pretty soon she had flown to the USA for tournaments in Scottsdale, Indian Wells and Key Biscayne. The latest American adventure began badly and ended tragically. Henin lost two tie-breaks to little-known Spaniard Magui Serna, to find herself knocked out of Scottsdale in the very first round. At Indian Wells she was soon cruising against her compatriot Kim Clijsters, and took the first set 6-1, but she suddenly lost momentum and watched her Belgian rival take away a match that should have been hers. Clijsters was probably as surprised as anyone to win the final two sets with such ease, 6-3, 6-4. Now the Ericsson Open at Key Biscayne was the last American stage upon which Justine might salvage some pride.

The tournament began well enough. Henin gained a bye in the first round and brushed aside Elena Bovina 6-2, 6-2 in the second. Her Miami hotel base was proving a happy one – until she received a call from home. The faltering voice she heard on the other end of the line belonged to Thomas, her brother. The young man to whom she had been closest, before she met Pierre-Yves and he met Vanessa, sounded strange. Justine must have felt conflicting emotions as she began to listen. This was Thomas, who had put his studies and career on hold to give her company and support during sensitive years at the tennis academy in Mons; it was also the same Thomas who had perhaps raised the first and most passionate objections to Pierre-Yves and his attitude almost a year earlier. The phone call was a cry for help. Something terrible had happened to Thomas, arguably the worst thing that can happen to any man. His six-week-old son, Emilien, had died suddenly. Justine's nephew, the infant she had never held or known, had fallen victim to lung failure.

The baby's grandfather, Jose, revealed the background to this bleak moment. He told me: 'Thomas had woken at about four in the morning, looked at his baby and, seeing immediately that something was seriously wrong, he had rushed him to the hospital. By seven o'clock I had received a phone call from Thomas and he sounded distraught.' Fearing the worst Jose had gone immediately to the hospital, but the baby was dead. Thomas fell into his arms and the very first thing he said was: 'I want Justine to come back.'

Jose warned Thomas not to call her, that she might not say the things he needed to hear, that she would not be there for him as he had been for her in the past. He warned him it might cause him even more pain. But Thomas made the call anyway, he felt he had to.

However, Jose was wrong, because Thomas heard the words of comfort he had hoped to hear from his sister. He recalled: 'The initial conversation was very good, considering everything. She said she wanted to be near me. I asked her to come. I said that we were waiting for her. Her reply was that she had a match to play the following day and she would have to see.'

For whatever reason – perhaps because the bereavement coincided with a crucial moment in her career, perhaps because she felt obliged to respect her professional commitments, or perhaps because of other outside pressures – Justine did not pull out of the tournament and return home. You can almost understand her dilemma. Her relationship with Thomas had changed significantly, their lives had moved apart and they were no longer close like before. She knew she was on the way to making her tennis dreams come true, but suddenly a fresh tragedy threatened to pull her back into the old world, the old order, the old arguments. She tried to focus on her tennis instead, supported by Carlos Rodriguez, but perhaps her brother's call was preying on her mind, for she lost 3-6, 1-6 to a little-known Italian called Tathiana Garbin.

As far as the Henin family were concerned, there should have been no dilemma at all – and no match against Garbin. Justine's kind-hearted grandfather, Alphonse, summed up their feelings at the height of the feud when he sighed and said: 'Thomas was there with his son dead. And she told him she had a tennis match the next day. As if a tennis match can count in life like a death.' So the Henin family grieved and tried to come to terms with the latest merciless twist of fate.

Justine remained determined to climb to the top of the game. In early May, she played in the Eurocard Ladies German Open in Berlin. She started well beating the South African Joanette Kruger and then homegrown girl Jana Kandarr to set up a clash with the mighty Venus Williams in the third round. It was their first meeting and Williams, then world number two, didn't know quite what she was letting herself in for. Despite being dwarfed by the American, Justine pulverised Venus 6-1 in a truly breathtaking first set. Before the far taller girl could recover, she found herself having to shake hands and take a shower. Henin had won the second set 6-4 and the result sent shockwaves through tennis, putting Justine's name on everyone's lips for perhaps the first time. To her credit, Venus wasn't about to make excuses. In fact she made a remark as generous as it was prophetic. 'If Justine played like this every day, she would be number one in the world.'

Henin accepted that she had played like a number one to register 'such a big win'. As for reaching top spot one day, she said: 'I am 18 and have many years before me. I must wait. Today was a big success, but I must become more consistent. But it works well at the moment. I played wonderful tennis. I hit many balls to the middle of the court, which Venus doesn't particularly like.'

In the quarter-final Henin claimed her second German victim, Miriam Schnitzer, with a comfortable 6-4, 6-2 workout. Now it was time to face another big-name American, Jennifer Capriati. Justine raced to a 6-2 first set win, but Capriati battled back to take the second 6-4. Henin led 2-1 in the third when a sprained right ankle ended her campaign. Playing with painful injuries would become a regular occurrence for both girls in their upcoming meetings.

Meanwhile, her paternal grandparents, Alphonse and Jeanne, continued to watch Justine's career progress. Since Justine was still so young, they remained convinced that one day she would be reconciled with her family. Since tennis was her chosen course, and her talent God-given, Alphonse and Jeanne were still prepared, in the early summer of 2001, to give her time to grow up. They continued to follow her big matches on television, cheering her on, trying to support her as she took on the world.

The next sporting test for their granddaughter was Roland Garros, Justine's own theatre of dreams. The French Open waited in all its glory, and Justine already felt it was her destiny to win it one day. Although Alphonse knew that a tennis match could not count in life like a death, it was also true that the tension surrounding a tennis match could become so infectious, through the power of television, that even elderly people watching in other countries could sometimes be left in mortal danger.

CHAPTER 7

ALPHONSE AND THE CHOKING HAZARD

IT WAS LIKE A DREAM. JUSTINE HAD STORMED INTO THE 2001 French Open semi-final, and she was playing well enough to go all the way. Now a formidable and familiar figure stood in her path. For Justine's opponent would be her oldest rival and compatriot, Kim Clijsters.

The bubbly blonde girl from the Dutch-speaking north of Belgium was a year younger than Justine, and had been part of her tennis life for as long as she could remember. They had been trying to outgun each other since they were small children; and even back then they must have felt the pressure, because both girls had been tipped for greatness by their respective supporters.

Henin and Clijsters had first met in the semi-final of the junior or 'Preminiemen' branch of the Memorial Vandewiele, a respected tournament held each summer in Ostend. Jose cast his mind back: 'I think Justine was only nine or ten, so Kim would have been eight, even though the category was 10-12 years old. The sets they played were four games instead of six. Otherwise it was normal tennis. The match drew a big crowd because there were a lot of Flemish people following Kim, whom we hadn't heard of. Clijsters was the great new hope for the Flemish, who stood on one side of the court. On our side there were lots of French-speaking people, because Justine had already built a reputation for herself as a very good player.

'So this match became quite an occasion, especially when you consider how young the girls were, with Flemish on one side and Walloons (French-speaking Belgians) on the other. But Justine didn't mind the pressure, because she took the first set 4-0. Then do you know what happened? Kim claimed she was injured, and that was it. Maybe she felt the strain. The strange thing is she was suddenly fit enough to play in a doubles match an hour later.'

Even so, Justine knew that Clijsters was a year younger, and suspected she would be a constant threat as they grew older. Jose told me: 'Justine was worried from the start about Kim's talent, and I had to reassure her that it would be something she could learn to deal with. I told her not to worry. I told her just to accept that Clijsters would always be a big rival. I told her she would probably have a picture of Justine on her wall as motivation. So accept the challenge, I said. Accept it — and then beat her.'

Nine years had passed since the first clash, a period during which they had sometimes been adversaries and sometimes roommates, depending on whether they had been playing in singles competitions against each other, or representing Belgium as part of the same team. Now they had both hit the big-time, just as everyone had predicted. There was no space for friendship any more, there was too much at stake. This Roland Garros semi-final was far and away the most important tennis match either young woman had played; and although they knew each other's games inside out, this occasion might show the world which exciting prospect had the big-match temperament to go with her amazing ability. The venue for the semi-final wasn't the sacred Court Central, but the other great showcourt of Roland Garros, the Court Suzanne Lenglen.

Henin wanted to appear on the biggest stage of all, and came out like a whirlwind and Clijsters had no answer. Justine had taken a 5-1 lead in the first set almost before she had broken sweat, and she was playing the sort of crushing tennis that is virtually impossible to counter. Then the heavens opened and the rain fell, giving her opponent temporary respite. It didn't alter the course of that first set though, because when they resumed Justine closed out 6-2.

No one was more delighted back home than her 81-year-old maternal grandfather, Georges Rosiere. Georges and Justine were closer than ever, and his attitude to Pierre-Yves was the key. Although he had initially been as upset as anyone that his granddaughter was spending less time with her relatives and more time with Hardenne, he had soon understood what the young man meant to her. Unlike other men in the Henin family, Georges had accepted Pierre-Yves, and many a Sunday was spent with the three of them together in the Rosiere home, laughing and joking. Georges could see that Pierre-Yves made Justine happy. Indeed the only thing that could rival her love for him was her ambition to win Roland Garros. Now she was on the verge of the final, just one step short of achieving her dream.

At the end of the rue de Grottes in Justine's home village of Han-sur-Lesse, her other surviving grandparents, Alphonse and Jeanne, were cheering 'JuJu', as she was affectionately known, with equal passion. Family recriminations were on hold, this was a huge moment in their granddaughter's life and hardly one to be ignored, whatever their feelings about her recent behaviour. Jean-Marie, Jose and Jean-Paul, their three sons, were with Alphonse and Jeanne, willing Justine to victory. They cheered as though they were in the Paris stadium with her, and reached out with her to seize the dream they had all worked towards. As she broke Clijsters again in the second set to lead 4-2, a place in the final seemed all but guaranteed. What could possibly go wrong now?

Justine had been cruising and she took her foot off the pedal, tightening slightly as she saw the finishing tape. Three break points were squandered when a little more ruthlessness would have ended the argument once and for all. No matter, a few nerves were only natural with so much at stake, and she merely needed to regain her composure in order to close out the match. And yet that composure, together with the mental strength which had put her in this winning position in the first place, simply drifted away. Henin's performance was growing weaker by the second. Clijsters must have sensed what everyone could see with their own eyes – Justine was 'choking' and due to the doubts in Justine's head, Kim was allowed to battle back from nowhere to take the second set 7-5. She and everyone else knew she should really have been in the locker room, having wished Justine good luck for the final. Henin's magic had evaporated along with her self-belief. Try as she might, she couldn't find a foothold in the final set either. It was excruciating to watch.

Back in Belgium, the blood pressure rose among the family elders. They simply couldn't believe what they were watching. Georges Rosiere knew better than anyone what victory would mean for Justine if she could turn this ominous tide. His daughter, JuJu's mother, had shared the little girl's dream of Roland Garros glory while she lived, and for Justine to fulfil that dream in honour of Francoise would be satisfying beyond measure. By the same token, to let it slip away would be devastating on a very personal level; so Justine fought desperately to prevent that night-mare from happening. Still nothing seemed to go her way; and Georges would have shared the same sick, sinking feeling which was growing in the stomachs of all Henin's closest supporters.

Down on the rue de Grottes, Justine's other grandfather, Alphonse, had watched with horror as Justine's game disintegrated. He willed her to play to her true potential, as she had done less than an hour earlier. He played every point with her, as if trying to lend her what was left of his own fading strength. But the more Justine's form slipped away, the more anxious Alphonse became, and his nor-mally smiling face was filled with tension.

Tennis should never be a matter of life and death, but its drama can claim victims beyond the arena itself. As Justine fought and failed to hold her serve when it mattered in Roland Garros, the frustration back in Belgium became intolerable. Finally, Henin was put out of her misery by her arch-rival, who had produced one of the great French Open comebacks to take the final set 6-3. The dream was shattered.

Justine tried to collect her thoughts and fight her despair. Even after such a soul-destroying defeat, she was anxious to understand what had happened. Hadn't she said earlier in the tournament that she had learned how to play pivotal points in a match? What could she offer by way of explanation, if she were asked why she had choked with victory almost in her grasp?

In Han-sur-Lesse the Henin family were carrying out a similar inquest into what had gone wrong. Alphonse recalled: 'Jean-Marie, Justine's uncle, was particularly animated, to the point of being angry because she had lost. I was agitated as well, because she should have won it, and we were arguing about what had gone wrong. Then something happened to me. Suddenly I was staggering around and slurring my words, talking as though I were drunk. Jean-Paul's wife, Clelia, thought I really was drunk.' Jean-Paul soon realised something was seriously wrong with his father. He helped Alphonse gently into his car and rushed him to hospital in nearby Dinant. Jean-Paul was frightened by now and remembered later: 'I was driving along and he was talking rubbish about how pretty the Christmas lights were. It was June . . .'

Unaware of the makings of yet another family tragedy, Justine began her post-match press conference, knowing at least that she had reached the top 10 for the first time. 'It was almost perfect,' she began wistfully, as she looked back on the match. 'But mentally I was becoming weak . . . it was in my head. At this time I perhaps thought nothing could happen.'

Had she felt that her late mother was with her in spirit, and victory was meant to be, so that she sat back, believing that destiny would do the rest? Momentarily she had perhaps forgotten the golden rule, that you carve out your own destiny in sport. Clijsters had needed only a moment, a small flicker of hope, to demonstrate that painful truth on the day.

Having already squandered one winning position in a less important match against Kim at Indian Wells, there lurked in Justine the suspicion that she had begun to develop a mental block when it came to beating her compatriot. 'Maybe I have problems concluding matches against Kim,' she conceded. 'If it had been another player as my opponent, I might have won 6-2, 6-2 . . . Playing a player from your country is not easy . . . It's not a question of being friends with her. It's simply that I was on the point of doing something great, to be in the finals of a Grand Slam tournament. Maybe if it had been somebody else, it would have been easier.'

And not only for Justine. At that precise moment, Alphonse was fighting for his life. The doctors in Dinant quickly identified the problem – blood clots on the brain. Due to that early, accurate, diagnosis, they managed to save him. Although it would take several weeks in hospital before he recovered sufficiently to leave his bed, Alphonse was at least alive. He had been down and almost out, but he had found enough of the famous Henin willpower to survive his ordeal. He couldn't speak properly, and it would be a while before the ability to form clear words returned. But he had plenty of time to reflect upon the dangers of tennis.

For Justine, tennis was so central to her life that any perceived weakness in her game, either physical or psychological, was intolerable. She talked in depth with her coach about the Clijsters jinx and what had gone wrong at Roland Garros. Carlos and his player were determined to ensure that it would never happen again. Within 48 hours

Justine was back in training, on a synthetic surface in Belgium. It was the closest she could find in her own country to the grass of Wimbledon, and it also gave her a chance to visit her grandfather Alphonse, as he began to make his slow recovery.

Alphonse smiled as he remembered: 'She came to the hospital in Dinant with her aunt, my daughter Genevieve. We talked, although I couldn't really get many words out. I didn't say it had happened because of the match. I didn't want to hurt her.'

Perhaps humbled by the pain of Roland Garros, however, Justine's attitude to her father softened for a while. Jose recalled: 'She was down after the defeat to Clijsters and she came to see me twice. She even brought along Pierre-Yves. We went to see some houses in the country near Rochefort, a neighbouring town, with a view to their buying one, and we got on well. She was going to play a grass-court tournament in Rosmalen, Holland, and said she would call me from there. She didn't, but of course it was nearly time for Wimbledon then. I didn't call her or push it, I was just happy that we had enjoyed that contact together away from tennis. I heard later from someone that she had told her coach how much happier she felt after our meeting.'

Maybe Jose thought those meetings went better than they actually did, or perhaps Pierre-Yves was less enthusiastic about the prospect of having Justine's father back in his life than she was. After all, when a young man is looking at houses with his fiancée, he doesn't necessarily want his future father-in-law offering advice on what might make the best choice as the future marital home. Later Justine looked back on occasional attempts like this to communicate with her family during the long feud: 'We tried but it was tough.'

Whatever the reality behind these tentative gestures from Justine, Jose certainly felt new hope that he might soon be involved in the happy couple's wedding plans after all. He dared to imagine that the worst of the destructive family rift might finally be over. What he didn't realise, as Wimbledon approached, was that the feud was only just beginning.

CHAPTER 8

'PAPY' GEORGES, NUMBER ONE FAN

GEORGES ROSIERE COULDN'T RESIST THE TEMPTATION TO call. Justine Henin had annihilated the powerful Conchita Martinez 6-1, 6-0 in the 2001 Wimbledon quarter-final, and no one felt prouder of her ability to bounce back than Georges. The scoreline bordered on humiliation for the poor Spaniard; but what thrilled Justine's family and friends, so soon after the nightmare of Roland Garros, was that she had faced a big occasion in a Grand Slam and seized her opportunity with both hands. Indeed Henin's game, already known for its punishing backhand, had shown a new dimension; for the experts had noticed how Justine's forehand had shone equally brightly during this fearsome demolition. When her game was flowing on both sides, the gritty little Belgian girl was simply unstoppable, and her performance was causing genuine excitement.

Ironically she had nearly left Wimbledon unnoticed, when a far less formidable test on one of the outside courts had almost put paid to her campaign a few days earlier. In Henin's second-round match against Kristie Boogert she had trailed 5-7, 1-4, with a break point against her. But she had clung on for dear life and this time she had watched her opponent choke. With ruthless efficiency, Justine had hit back to take the match 5-7, 7-5, 6-2. And now, after thrashing Martinez, Justine stood only two steps away from Wimbledon glory.

The prospect of another Grand Slam semi-final, so soon after she had choked in Paris, could have been daunting had she allowed herself to entertain any negative thoughts. Instead she told reporters confidently: 'Now I have more experience. I will enjoy this moment more . . . I was 6-2, 4-2 up in Paris and I didn't win the match. Maybe if I have the possibility here, I will not make the same mistake.'

Justine was enjoying her moment already when 'Papy' Georges enhanced it with a call from back home. She loved every minute as he congratulated her on what she had done so far, and underlined his faith in her as she prepared for her next challenge. While many tried and failed to speak to Justine at this special time, the unconditional love Georges had always shown his granddaughter meant that his was a precious name and number in her phone. There was nothing emotionally draining or complicated about talking to a dear old man who had supported her so sensitively since the death of her mother, his daughter. Perhaps her favourite relation left in this world, Georges was her last direct link to her beloved mother. The man she called 'Papy' could amuse her with his boyish enthusiasm, while at the same time offering her a wise old man's perspective during these heady times in London.

The conversation must have been particularly sweet. It was always an added pleasure for Justine to know how much happiness her success brought 'Papy', whose wife Bearthe had died of cancer many decades earlier. Doubtless he realised, like everyone else, that 'JuJu' was now on the verge of a truly glittering career. She would become a genuine contender for every Grand Slam she played, and surely it was only a matter of time before she took the biggest titles. For all he knew, that breakthrough might come in the next few days. Both Georges and Justine knew what her triumphs would have meant to her mother too. In many ways she was still the driving force behind Justine's relentless climb towards the summit of world tennis. And maybe, from somewhere up above them, Francoise was savouring these moments just like her father and daughter. It was a thought they would have enjoyed sharing.

As she prepared for her semi-final against the high-flying American, Jennifer Capriati, Justine was invited to reflect upon the frightening pace of her improvement. She was asked: 'If someone had told you at the beginning of the year that you would be in two Grand Slam semi-finals this year, what would you have said to them?'

Justine admitted: 'I wouldn't have believed them, for sure, because I was ranked 45 at the beginning of the year. I was 100 one year ago. So everything was so fast.'

In order to reach the Wimbledon final, she would need to convince herself that she deserved this success and had a genuine right to be there. Perhaps Jennifer Capriati picked up on a sense of disorientation in her opponent after such a meteoric rise in 2001. At any rate, the accomplished favourite, who had won both Grand Slams so far that year, strode onto Centre Court and began to demolish Justine, much as Henin had obliterated Martinez in the previous match. Capriati was faster than ever, despite her chunky physique, while Henin struggled to read the bounce on grass. Justine was also suffering from a horrible blister on her right foot. The added distraction sealed her first-set fate, and she lost 2-6.

Justine even thought about quitting at that point, because the pain from her foot was so bad. The match was beginning to look disappointingly one-sided when she fell behind 2-1 in the second set, and the impressive Capriati appeared to be on the verge of an amazing Grand Slam hat-trick.

Back in Belgium, arguably the most important person in Justine's life sat shell-shocked in the Rochefort Tennis Club, where she had once played day and night as a six-year-old. Pierre-Yves Hardenne (who was not in London due to tennis coaching commitments) had attracted the attention of the local media while watching his fiancée struggle, and they photographed him in various states of anguish. As the semi-final went on, the cameras caught his face in such contortions that it seemed he too was experiencing Justine's pain. Limbs flailed and their young owner was clearly helpless with frustration – having given up any attempt at maintaining his cool, he was an open book, and threw his hands up in horror at what he was seeing. A second dream seemed to be evaporating in the space of a few weeks.

Not far away, Georges Rosiere and Alphonse Henin, the elders of Justine's family, must have felt their pulses quicken once again. After what had happened to him last time, however, Alphonse tried to take a step back from the drama he could see unfolding on his television screen.

Across the English Channel, Justine wasn't quite ready to be labelled the 'nearly girl' of 2001, or dismissed as a 'choker' who crumbled whenever a Grand Slam final appeared on the horizon. By now she had called the trainer so that her blister could be treated. A new bandage worked wonders for the mind, even if the foot still didn't feel too good. And the time-out gave her time to reflect upon Roland Garros, and how she had vowed to bounce back. Justine couldn't quit now, she wouldn't. She thought back to Berlin, where she had been on the verge of beating Capriati before an injured ankle had denied her. Henin knew she was good enough, if only she could start to turn the tide.

A few well-placed shots gave her an all-important foothold in that second set, and suddenly Justine was beginning to play her normal game again. Pierre-Yves saw the transformation from the clubhouse in Rochefort, and a glimmer of hope returned to his staring eyes. Capriati began to look uncertain, and it was Henin's turn to take advantage. Fighting with everything she had, the underdog hit back to take the second set 6-4.

Georges and Alphonse were ecstatic as they watched from their homes and waited to see if their granddaughter could complete the comeback. Meanwhile Jose Henin strolled into the Rochefort Tennis Club to create a potentially volatile mix there. Undaunted by the prospect of viewing the rest of the match in close proximity to Pierre-Yves, the young man who had turned his world upside down, Jose made a point of supporting his daughter with equal vigour. Regulars at the Rochefort club waited with interest to see whether the fireworks in their bar would match the epic clash developing over the water.

Back at Wimbledon, Justine's adrenalin was clearly pumping like never before. She had gained the upper hand,

and Capriati was showing how fragile she too could be when placed under such massive pressure. The English crowd was on Henin's side as they sensed an upset. Justine broke again, and soon she was on that dangerous and deceptive home straight, the one that had proved too much for her in Paris. From there she could almost touch a Grand Slam final. Would she reach out again, only to lose her balance and watch the dream drift away?

In Belgium, Georges must have sensed that Justine looked more determined to meet the challenge set out before her. Alphonse must have suspected it too, though for him the priority was simply to get through the match in one piece, whatever the result. Meanwhile at opposite ends of the Rochefort clubhouse, Jose and Pierre-Yves held their breath. Although they were only on uneasy speaking terms, the two men were feeling exactly the same excitement now. Separately, they willed the girl they loved not to tighten or weaken.

The desolation of defeat against Clijsters was still a fresh and vivid memory for Justine. She used it. She would not release her stranglehold, even with victory so close, because to do so would invite a similar outcome. Point by crushing point, she squeezed all remaining hope out of Capriati, until the scoreboard read 2-6, 6-4, 6-2. The comeback was complete, her mission that day accomplished with the sort of deadly finish that had previously been lacking. Justine Henin, and not the overwhelming favourite, would play in the Wimbledon final.

Pierre-Yves was simply ecstatic by now, and the cameras captured his joy. Jose also felt immeasurable pride in his daughter's courage, and hopeful for the future as never before. With that in mind, he walked up to Pierre-Yves and shook him by the hand. It was a small but extraordinary gesture, almost one of conciliation. Jose understood that Pierre-Yves was in pole position now where his daughter's affections were concerned. He seemed to sense that this semi-final win was more their triumph than his, since he had played only a minor part in his daughter's recent life. The handshake suggested that he was prepared to accept the new order of things, in return perhaps for a little consideration. If Pierre-Yves wasn't exactly warm, he appeared to accept the olive branch for what it was. But he was probably already thinking about how he could get to Wimbledon in time for the final, and put his teaching commitments at a tennis summer school on hold.

Meanwhile, Justine was fielding a question about the reaction back home. She said: 'I suppose it's unbelievable in Belgium. I don't want to have any contacts with Belgium now because, you know, I have an important match on Saturday. After that, for sure, I will go back to Belgium. I will feel it a lot. I am so happy for the Belgian people, too.'

But when she said she didn't want any contact with Belgium, Justine didn't mean Pierre-Yves. And she would of course make a further exception for 'Papy' Georges. 'I called him after I beat Capriati,' she later revealed. 'He was so happy that I'd made it to the final, so proud.'

CHAPTER 9
THE WAITING GAME

JUSTINE MAY NOT HAVE WANTED CONTACT WITH HER father in the build-up to her first Wimbledon final, against the fearsome American, Venus Williams; but Jose wanted contact with Justine, albeit indirectly. He explained: 'I called her coach, Carlos Rodriguez, because I wanted to pass on my best wishes to my daughter for the Wimbledon final and I also congratulated him, as a coach, for getting her there. But there was something else on my mind too. On her way to the final, he had been holding informal press conferences with Belgian journalists and telling them what an achievement it had been for Justine to get that far, after all she had been through at home. So I told him to stop talking as if her life at home had been so bad. It wasn't true, I told him; and if it had been that way, we wouldn't have enjoyed seeing each other just a few weeks ago.'

Rodriguez has since revealed that he deliberately kept Justine's father on the line during a phone call at around this time. He told the *Sunday Times*: 'I had a long conversation with him, deliberately long. I wanted to keep him talking to see where his thoughts would lead. And sure enough, it was the same old story – complaints about Pierre-Yves and the desire to interfere with her life again. So I warned them what to expect and, unhappily, I was proved correct.'

Jose disputed that version of the conversation, which took place around the time I first met him. Although there may simply have been a misunderstanding between the two men, the Rodriguez account certainly didn't sit comfortably with the sentiments Jose expressed to me, face to face. To me he made it clear that he had learned from the breakdown of his relationship with Justine; that he wanted to be positive in future without being pushy; that he would go to watch her matches again only if she invited him; that the father-daughter relationship would thrive again only outside the world of tennis. Such a change of approach was hard to convey to Justine, however, when her inner circle was so protective and difficult to penetrate.

After her semi-final victory over Capriati, Henin had said of Rodriguez: 'We've been working together for five years now. I was 14 when I started with him. If I didn't have Carlos, I wouldn't be here today because I think he's a coach, a friend, he is everything for me. I can talk with him about my personal life or my tennis life. I think he knows what to say to me for myself.'

Did Carlos think it would be better for Justine to focus on her tennis without the family complications that had apparently dragged her down in the past? Was Justine herself anxious to maintain the existing distance between father and daughter? The problem with perpetuating the feud, however, was that it was bound to create media interest around the world.

Justine had been relatively unknown in England until she reached the Wimbledon final, but the exploits of the battling Belgian underdog had captured the hearts of the tennis-loving British public that week. Rumours of a rift between father and daughter had reached London too, and the *Mail on Sunday* sent me to Belgium with three objectives: to locate Jose, persuade him to open his heart on the breakdown of his relationship with his daughter and then, if possible, watch the Wimbledon final with him. It was a big favour to ask of Justine's estranged father on such a difficult weekend for him. And although no one could know it at the time, life was about to become much harder for the entire family, the tennis star included. But he agreed to meet me at the Rochefort Tennis Club, and immediately set about sending out bridge-building messages of the sort that contrasted sharply with the subsequent claims by Rodriguez.

The day before Justine's Wimbledon final Jose told me: 'I saw Justine three weeks ago, and she told her coach afterwards that it made her feel better. I fully accept the relationship between Justine and Pierre-Yves now. We all take time to adapt to new situations. But if they get married in the next year or so, I believe it is my place as her father to be there with her. When she comes back to Belgium after Wimbledon, we will speak about tennis for no more than a minute. Then we must change the subject. Things will be much better between us again. I want to believe that will happen. But it must happen away from tennis. I don't want to be on Centre Court for her Wimbledon final.'

At least, on the eve of the Wimbledon final, Carlos and Jose were in agreement on one issue: they knew it would be better if Jose stayed away. That didn't mean he would remain silent, though. Just as Carlos and Justine were using the media to their advantage, Jose recognised that it was also his right to do so. Perhaps that was partly why we hit it off so well; and Friday slowly faded into a haze of strong local beers, including several bottles of 'Trappiste', the Rochefort brew first concocted by the region's inventive monks.

Introductions to family friends and fellow villagers followed, as did more local beers and a barbecue. Jose poured out his heart and revealed some of the frustrations that had led to the feud. He seemed to like having a total outsider to talk to for a change; the intricacies of the closely interwoven lives above the famous caves of Han-sur-Lesse were sometimes as claustrophobic as the darkness that lay below. We talked for what seemed like half the night, and shook hands on a firm agreement to watch the final together the following day.

Sure enough, Jose was waiting at his house in the pretty little village of Hamarenne, just outside Han-sur-Lesse, on Saturday morning. But sadly there was to be no women's final between Venus Williams and Justine Henin that Saturday, only frustrating, monotonous rain. At least Justine would have her coach and her boyfriend close at hand during the long and agonising wait. Although Jose suspected, rightly or wrongly, that both men had done much to bring about his estrangement from Justine, he also knew they would be a source of strength and inspiration to her on the biggest day of her professional life. Though they couldn't hold her hand in the loneliness of the Wimbledon locker room, their proximity, along with Justine's faithful aunt Genevieve, would keep her feeling as composed as humanly possible.

Perhaps those left back in Belgium felt the mounting tension even more keenly. For years, Justine's loved ones had dared to dream that her talent would lead her to a moment like this. Now the famously unpredictable elements on the other side of the Channel had conspired to prevent that moment from arriving. For Justine's maternal grandfather, Georges Rosiere, that tension was becoming unbearable. His bond with Justine was unique, perhaps because only Georges could sustain her with stories of her late mother's childhood and teenage years, giving new life to the memory of Francoise for the girl who had been denied her beloved parent since the age of 12.

However, although Georges had followed Justine's meteoric rise with all the enthusiasm of a teenager, he no longer inhabited a teenager's body; and the stresses and strains of his fanatical support were starting to take their toll. The outcome of the match would be entirely beyond his control, and now the weather was delaying Justine's fate in a way that could only have increased his sense of helpless frustration. He must have imagined Justine sitting in the locker room, growing more nervous by the minute, and that would have served to make him more agitated.

'Papy' knew all about the dangers of getting caught up in Justine's career. He was only too aware that his 'opposite number' – Alphonse Henin – had almost paid the ultimate price for supporting her too passionately at the last tournament. At a time like this, it was best to try to take a step back, and perhaps even concentrate on another activity. Towards the end of the day, Georges sensibly wondered whether he might be better off going out to mow the lawn, since the length of the grass was at least something over which he could have some influence. Tantalisingly, Tim

Henman and Goran Ivanisevic were able to step out for a cameo appearance in their rain-delayed men's semi-final before the heavens opened again, and the announcement was finally made: the women's final would now take place on Sunday. Having stared at his television screen for the best part of a day, Georges Rosiere's frustration was complete. He rose to his feet and headed for the garden.

In Hamarenne, I had already written a 'holding piece' for the *Mail on Sunday*, detailing the Henin family feud from Jose's point of view. With a lack of action on court, the story was assured a good 'show' in the following day's paper, taking up some of the space that would otherwise have been occupied by the match. Everyone had started to relax again, looking forward as we were to a sociable evening and the prospect of an enthralling final the next day.

An unexpected knock on the door changed everything. It was answered by Jose, who found himself confronted with the pale, anxious face of his eldest son, David. Although he had been so friendly the night before, poor David seemed less than pleased to find the reporter from the barbecue sitting comfortably on his father's sofa. He clearly had something important and deeply private to say. Even at this awkward moment, the 27-year-old was too polite to ask his father to show me the door. And before I could offer to leave of my own accord, he ushered Jose and Sarah into the kitchen and delivered his grim news.

'It's Georges,' said David simply. 'He's had a heart attack. They've taken him to hospital but it doesn't look good. They may not be able to save him.'

CHAPTER 10
THE TRAGIC SECRET

SARAH WAS ALREADY INCONSOLABLE. I HAD NO IDEA WHAT was happening until she ran to her room in tears. Jose put me in the picture, on the condition that I promised not to write a story that night about the latest misfortune to hit Justine's ill-fated relatives. Journalists have a rather perverse ability to ignore the consequences of the stories they write. 'Tragedy Strikes Wimbledon Finalist' might have made a powerful headline on the *Mail on Sunday*'s back page. However, no one with a conscience would have wanted a 19-year-old girl to find out about her grandfather's heart attack by glancing at the back of a London newspaper – especially not on the biggest day of her life. I therefore readily gave Jose the assurance he required, and left the Henin family with their next excruciating dilemma: when to tell Justine the sad news.

They knew how much Georges would have hated the idea that what had happened to him might in any way ruin Justine's chances of taking the Wimbledon title. If they broke the news to her before the match, it might well harm her performance. But if they let her play not knowing, how would she react afterwards? Worse still, if the news leaked out and she got wind of the story through other sources, she might never forgive those who had tried to protect her from the truth.

Calls to Carlos Rodriguez suggested that the decision had effectively been taken out of Jose's hands already. His sisters, Francoise in Belgium and Genevieve in London, had debated the matter with Rodriguez. Even at this highly sensitive time for the family, the ultimate decision seemed to rest with Carlos. But on this occasion Justine's father actually agreed with her mentor: she should be told about Georges only after the final on Sunday, whatever his condition by then.

Just hours before the rain-delayed 2001 women's final at Wimbledon, Jose Henin was woken by the chirpy ring tone of his mobile phone. It was the call he had been dreading. Although Georges Rosiere had clung bravely to life all night, he had passed away at six o'clock that morning. Sadly, one of Justine's biggest fans had not lived long enough to see how valiantly she would fight on her big day.

With Sarah's blessing, Jose decided to join the bigger crowd to watch his elder daughter play Venus Williams. After the trauma of the previous 24 hours, he wanted to escape the sombre atmosphere in his house and tap into the positive energy now being generated by the local community. A giant screen had been erected in Rochefort's leisure centre. Some six hundred people were expected to inject new life into the party that had fallen flat the previous day.

Georges would not have wanted his death to spoil Justine's historic Sunday. There would be time for mourning after Wimbledon; but now the match Rosiere had spent his last day on earth waiting to see would finally get under way, with his granddaughter up against a tennis giant in every sense. Somehow it seemed right that all the energies of the living should go towards willing her dream to come true. Georges would have liked things that way, and Jose knew it.

Before he joined the throng in the leisure centre, Jose took a morning stroll around Rochefort. Acquaintances weren't slow to come up to the local man whose daughter was the talk of the town. They congratulated him on what Justine had already achieved and they assured him that they were with her all the way. Dutifully he smiled and thanked them for their support.

In every shop window there were posters emblazoned with the same emphatic message: 'VAS-Y, JUJU!' – 'Come on Justine!' The townsfolk had claimed her as one of their own. In some ways she was now more their daughter than his. To Jose, this hero-worship seemed a little bizarre. He was the focal point for adulation by proxy, father of a famous daughter who rarely talked to him. It was almost laughable.

The venue was filled with kegs of beer, fans dressed in crazy hats, decked out in the Belgian national colours of red, yellow and black – and scores of reporters. Some crept down the central aisle to grab a word with Jose before the match began. One tactlessly mentioned rumours of a fresh bereavement in the family. Somehow word of Georges' death had leaked out. Jose was alarmed to consider what the consequences might be over in London. But gradually he realised that the Belgian reporters had decided to join the growing, benevolent conspiracy to keep the news from

Justine before her final. Always a worrier, Jose feared the worst but eventually he declared: 'Once she's on Centre Court she'll be safe, at least until later.'

When Justine emerged from the locker room still smiling, we all knew we had done our bit. Jose looked immensely relieved because mentally his daughter seemed in reasonably good shape – which was more than could be said for Tim Henman. Britain's finest had crashed and burned minutes earlier against Goran Ivanisevic in front of his home crowd, a swift anti-climax to the stop-start men's semi-final. Now Henin had marched out with Venus for what appeared to be an even more obvious physical mismatch. Williams was six foot and one inch tall and weighed 160 pounds. Justine was five foot five inches (and three-quarters) and weighed 125 pounds. She had beaten Venus in Berlin; but this was grass and she would have to fight like never before if she wanted to pull off the upset many tennis fans wanted to see.

Henin, the girl who had looked so ready when she first came out for action, suddenly seemed stiff as she snatched at her shots, hesitated at vital moments and moved heavily around the court. As the underdog struggled to find her usual snappy rhythm, Venus imposed herself with a series of bludgeoning assaults, designed to shatter the confidence of the smaller girl. The favourite waged some psychological warfare too, the intensity of which took Justine aback, for all her own mental toughness. The Belgian girl would later admit: 'I felt a little intimidated because she kept giving me these strong, strange looks.'

Justine tried to fight back and there were glimmers of hope in that first set that she might soon find a way to hold her own. But every time she forced an opening, Venus slammed it shut with her supreme athleticism and relentless power. 'I don't understand it,' Jose Henin said as he watched his daughter lose the first set 1-6: 'she has always performed so well in finals.'

It was now or never; Justine could either find a way to play her best tennis or risk spending the rest of her life wondering what might have been. Typically, she came out for the second set and fought like a tiger. The ferocity of her returns, particularly on her famous backhand, seemed to shock her opponent. Venus, who had enjoyed such an ominous hold on the match just a few minutes earlier, was suddenly filled with uncharacteristic doubt.

In Belgium, the crowd leapt to its feet and Jose began to cheer the daughter who had all but disowned him. While the media cameras had been shoved almost into his face in order to capture his despair during the first set, now they caught the most animated gestures of his joyful support. In no time, Justine had broken the Venus serve that had previously looked so invincible, and closed out the second set 6-3, to cheers around Wimbledon's historic Centre Court. Another famous Henin comeback was in full flow, and in some ways this was a moral victory in itself.

As Justine said later: 'When you play a Grand Slam final, it's a big moment in your life. When I came back at one set all, it was a great moment for me.' Win or lose from here, she had demonstrated her fighting spirit and given the people back home something to shout about. Jose looked indescribably proud, and he knew how delighted Georges Rosiere would have been for his granddaughter too.

Henin was within touching distance of a Wimbledon title. What she had to do now, at all costs, was stay focused, and start the final set with as much venom as she had finished the second. But to maintain that sort of momentum against such a warrior of an opponent was easier said than done. Perhaps the effort she had already expended in order to draw level had taken too much out of her, especially when combined with the nervous energy used up in coping with the sheer enormity of the occasion. At any rate, just when JuJu needed to scrap like never before, it was Williams who found an extra gear. She broke Justine's serve immediately in that third and final set and never looked back, setting about her opponent with a series of punishing winners that left Justine looking punch-drunk.

In Rochefort, the hall fell silent. Try as she might to recover some form, Henin looked a spent force, her confidence destroyed. The crowd waited for the now-inevitable end with a touch of sadness. The match had turned from epic comeback to one-sided demolition. Venus Williams won Wimbledon 6-1, 3-6, 6-0.

The afternoon was about to get much worse for Justine. Later she hinted that she had known something was wrong by the way those closest to her were behaving, but had tried to suspend the suspicion. She said: 'That match was supposed to be a party but everyone I knew in the stands looked very sad. I knew it couldn't be for my match because I took Venus to three sets. I guessed something else was wrong.'

She faced the press after the final with a typically positive defiance. 'I will be number five in the world on Monday and this was one more experience. I will remember it all my life.' But Justine would soon have another, far sadder reason to remember that day. She couldn't be protected from the truth any longer, and was taken into a quiet room deep inside Wimbledon, where her entourage was waiting to break the terrible news about her 'Papy' Georges. She revealed later: 'Then they told me after my press conference – I had lost my grandfather that day. He was almost the last family member on my mother's side, and so it was very painful. He was 81 but he seemed in great shape and he drove to lots of my tournaments. The last time we spoke was when I called after I beat Capriati in the semis. He was so happy for me, so proud, and I'm glad he knew I made it to the final. He was always behind me and never judged my decisions. That was someone I love so much and I was very close to him.'

What could have been the greatest day of her life had ended in the worst way imaginable.

CHAPTER 11

GOODBYES AND HIGHS

JUSTINE HAD A ROYAL ESCORT BACK HOME TO THE FUNERAL. Prince Philippe and Princess Mathilde of Belgium had been supporting her at Wimbledon, and they flew home business class together. Despite the valiant efforts of the royals to keep her spirits up, Justine knew the days ahead would be painful and complicated. The funeral would bring her back into contact with people she had tried to leave behind, though not, as it turned out, with her father. Jose had already thought the situation through and decided that it would be better for all concerned if he didn't attend his father-in-law's funeral. Instead, he went to pay his respects to Georges Rosiere at the mortuary. That way there was one less reason for the ceremony to turn into a media circus.

What Justine didn't want was to be the centre of attention. However, certain photographers ignored her request for privacy during the funeral itself, and took pictures during moments of maximum distress. When the fuss had subsided, Justine and Pierre-Yves retreated to her local tennis club in Han-sur-Lesse, where he was holding summer-school classes. Only hours earlier she had played on Centre Court and had almost become queen of Wimbledon. Now she was back in touch with her tennis roots, to the delight of the local children, whose summer-school prospectus had never hinted at a meeting with one of the game's biggest new stars. Soon they were enjoying an impromptu tennis lesson in warm sunshine with one of the finest young players in the world.

Word reached Jose of what was happening, and he told me we could go down to the club to meet her. For all the supposed friction between them, Justine didn't seem displeased to see her father. She must have known that they would bump into each other at some stage on the visit. Even when Jose introduced his new journalist friend, she smiled politely and shook hands. Pierre-Yves, in contrast, glared across from the tennis court, pacing up and down like a caged tiger. But this moment belonged to just two people, and I stepped away to give them some space.

From a distance, Justine seemed relaxed and respectful to her father as they chatted; warm enough to encourage the belief, perhaps, that she might make some proper time in her busy schedule for her sole surviving parent. Jose told me later that he had taken the opportunity to express sorrow over what had happened to her 'Papy'. He also congratulated Justine on her performance at Wimbledon, and explained how he felt about their own relationship.

He claimed later: 'I made it clear, as we talked, face to face, that I never wanted to go back on the circuit. I just wanted us to be father and daughter. And she said of the previous trouble between us "if Mum had been alive, it would never have happened like this". I asked her if I could call her in a couple of days, and she said yes.'

Father and daughter talked for only a few precious minutes before she returned to Pierre-Yves, but Jose looked so much happier afterwards; it was as though a weight had been lifted from his shoulders. To an outsider, it appeared that his daughter had finally shown him the consideration he had been hoping for since before her extraordinary Wimbledon adventure. True, Justine was in a public place with a journalist standing not far away. By the end of the meeting, however, they seemed to have broken the ice again. Surely it hadn't been an act for anyone else's benefit?

Jose later took up the sad story of his follow-up phone call. 'I had hardly said a word when she stopped me and asked me what I had said to Carlos about going back on the circuit. I told her I never wanted to see another of her matches in person again, or have anything to do with the circuit, but she wasn't having it. She didn't believe me. So that brief, friendly exchange at the tennis club was the last time I saw her for a very long time.'

Justine wanted to look to the future, not the past. She was determined to enhance her growing reputation on the tennis court, and leave any personal problems behind. The perfect opportunity came in November 2001, when Belgium challenged for the Federation Cup, a competition thrown wide open by the withdrawal of the USA because of the events of 11 September that year. Henin, who was now ranked seventh in the world, and Kim Clijsters, who was above her in fifth position, would put their rivalry on hold and team up together. Joined by their compatriots, Laurence Courtois and Els Callens, they headed off for the tournament in Spain with high hopes.

Justine helped Belgium dispose of Germany 3-0 in a preliminary round with a 6-3, 6-1 victory over Martina

Muller. Then Australia was dismissed with surprising ease, again 3-0. The next test would be Spain, the host nation, and Justine had to play local favourite Conchita Martinez in front of a fiercely partisan crowd in Madrid. She took the first set 6-3, but the crowd went crazy when Martinez hit back to take the second 7-5. They were already celebrating wildly when Conchita raced to a 5-1 lead in the final set, and cheered loudly as a shell-shocked Justine served a fault. Although the Belgian girl was still staring defeat in the face, she had suddenly been given a very dangerous weapon – she was angry.

Justine released some of that anger in what everyone assumed would be the last few, defiant points that she could possibly win. In doing so she recaptured some of the timing that had gone missing at the end of the first set. With every successful shot Henin grew more and more determined to punish the Spanish crowd for the way in which they had taunted her. And as she gained a foothold in that final set, and began to break back, the crowd fell silent.

All the time Conchita and her supporters knew that one more game would seal victory. Yet that last hurdle suddenly seemed so high that Martinez looked incapable of clearing it, no matter how many half-chances she was given. Growing stronger by the minute, Justine shut the door on any recovery by her increasingly desperate opponent. Pretty soon there weren't even half-chances for Conchita to feed upon. Her game had collapsed in front of her own fans, and a merciless Henin took the last six games to complete the humiliation.

It was a victory that reinforced Justine's growing repu-tation as the comeback queen of world tennis, although she wasn't finished yet with her Spanish hosts. The 19-year-old said afterwards: 'I understand it's the host country and all the fans are here, but you have to respect the players. When you've got to make a second serve and the crowd are making all that noise, it's very difficult for the players. It's my first experience of this type of game and I just tried to focus. I understand the crowd, but it's not really proper behaviour.'

She needn't have worried about the behaviour of Spanish spectators during the final against Russia, because only 2,000 of them turned up to watch. Neither did Justine try to draw out the entertainment any longer than necessary. Her first set in the drubbing of Nadia Petrova took only 14 minutes, and she ran out a comfortable 6-0, 6-3 winner. With the help of Clijsters, tiny Belgium became champions of the world, defeating the mighty Russians 2-1 overall in the final. But it was Henin's victories which had been the highlight of that unlikely march to the title. Afterwards she said: 'It's great for a little country with two young players and a great team.'

It seemed that nothing could hold Justine back, whatever tragedies or feuds lurked behind the scenes. The stronger she became, and the more belief she developed in her own tennis ability, the more she appeared convinced that drastic tactics with regard to her family were entirely justified. The dramatic year of 2001 was ending on a high for Justine, though it wouldn't turn out that way for some of those who still loved her dearly.

CHAPTER 12
DEFINING FAMILY

OF ALL HER RELATIVES, ALIVE OR DEAD, JUSTINE MOST resembles Jeanne Henin, her grandmother. Although time had inevitably carved its mark on Jeanne's proud features, they still glowed with the same feisty spirit for which Justine was becoming famous. The pair had always been close, although perhaps less so since Justine had turned her back on her father. He was, after all, Jeanne's and Alphonse's son. Despite that complication, Justine hoped their relationship could be maintained, as did Jeanne and Alphonse, who prayed for an end to the family conflict.

Not long after her Federation Cup triumph, Justine was due to play an exhibition tournament with Kim Clijsters, Nathalie Tauziat, Amelie Mauresmo and Silvia Farina Elia at Ciney, in Belgium. Justine invited her surviving grand-parents, Alphonse and Jeanne, to attend. Understandably reluctant to do anything that might perhaps be interpreted as a betrayal of family members to whom Justine had recently given less consideration, Alphonse and Jeanne declined the invitation. Besides, Alphonse wasn't in the best of health, and it didn't seem wise to travel.

The decision wasn't meant to be a slap in the face for Justine in any way; they simply preferred to stay on neutral territory until the family tensions were resolved to everyone's satisfaction. Alphonse and Jeanne assumed that their decision would be respected for what it was: a sensible piece of diplomacy. Indeed, Jeanne took the trouble to explain things very carefully to Justine when she came round to their house in the centre of Han-sur-Lesse one day.

As Jeanne recalled later, at the height of the feud: 'She came to see us and I gave her my reasons. I said I didn't want to go into the world of tennis that had hurt us so much, and caused so much pain to the family. She seemed to accept our reasons. And when she left, she turned and waved. And she said these words – I'll never forget them: "Je vous adore." And I don't think we have seen her since. We don't even get a Christmas card from her any more.'

Justine seemed to have taken her grandparents' perfectly understandable decision as a firm declaration of where their loyalties lay. It also seemed that rather than risk their disapproval, or have to explain her attitude towards their son, her father, every time they met, Justine simply cut Alphonse and Jeanne out of her life too.

It seemed the wider feud could only end if Jose found a way to get through to his daughter and finally make lasting peace with her. He certainly tried, and repeated his plea for involvement some months before the wedding day by saying: 'My place should be at my daughter's side on the big day, walking her down the aisle. She did not see fit to give me her news personally, and I still don't even know if I'll be invited to the wedding at all. Even if I'm not invited, she has my best wishes. I'll send flowers.'

At the start of 2002, there was no chance of Jose getting close enough to his daughter to make a difference to her thinking, because she was on the other side of the world for the Australian Open. A familiar pattern emerged, however, when she lost her quarter-final to the more highly ranked Kim Clijsters, 2-6, 3-6. Losing to Kim was becoming a habit, and she would need to get over that mental block if ever she was to achieve true greatness.

But tennis wasn't everything, as her father had realised. So when she returned to Belgium from Australia Jose decided to take the opportunity to visit her unannounced. He just wanted to talk to her as a father hoping to be involved in his daughter's wedding day. He wanted to show her that he had learned from his previous mistakes. After all, Jose continued to enjoy a good relationship with Justine's sister, Sarah. Why couldn't they all just be friends again, before it was too late? In pouring rain, Jose walked down the rue de la Station in Marloie and stopped by the butcher's shop, above which Justine shared a modest apartment with Pierre-Yves. He rang the doorbell, full of brave optimism for the future, despite the foul weather. He was confident that he could build some bridges and make life better for everyone if he was positive in his approach.

Pierre-Yves answered the door and Jose politely asked for his daughter.

'She doesn't want to see you any more,' was the abrupt reply.

Jose remembered this tense exchange vividly. 'It was as though he was really enjoying the moment,' he told me later. 'I asked if she could come down and tell me herself. He just stood there and repeated the words: "She doesn't want to see you any more." A terrible anger welled up inside me, because he looked so self-satisfied, and I must admit I felt like doing something I would later have regretted. But I kept my self-control and I simply walked away.'

Shattered and humiliated, Jose feared the worst. This had been a definitive moment in the deterioration of his relationship with his daughter, and yet she hadn't come down to tell him face to face how she felt. How much of this had been his daughter talking, and how much Pierre-Yves? He didn't know for sure, but he began to suspect that his chances of walking Justine down the aisle were very remote indeed.

If this severe attitude towards her family was supposed to remove all obstacles to tennis greatness, it didn't work – not yet, anyway. Henin crashed out of the French Open at the very first hurdle, falling victim to illness and a little-known Hungarian called Anika Kapros. At Wimbledon she had another wonderful run, and registered a first victory over Monica Seles, 7-5, 7-6 in the quarter-final. But standing in her way at the semi-final stage was the familiar, intimidating frame of Venus Williams, who dismissed Justine's latest challenge 3-6, 2-6 to end the dream for another year. When Henin didn't get any further than the last 16 at Flushing Meadows, two months later, even she had to admit that the wedding preparations were distracting her. She said: 'I know the marriage is not the best thing for my career. But I just did it for myself. I thought it was the right moment for me.'

Justine suffered two more crushing defeats to Clijsters only days before the biggest occasion of her life. On 8 November, Kim beat her 6-2, 6-1 in the quarter-final of the WTA Championships. 'Maybe that's the worst I've ever played against her,' she said. 'I was really tired. I completely forgot that I'm getting married next week, so that wasn't the reason for this.' Few agreed, especially when it happened again on 14 November, the Thursday before the wedding. The exhibition match in Brussels saw Clijsters run out a comfortable 6-1, 6-4 winner. Justine was almost reduced to the role of spectator, and even joined in the crowd's Mexican wave. To console her after her crushing defeat, Pierre-Yves, her knight-in-shining-armour, gave her a passionate kiss and a red rose. He was her family now, along perhaps with her aunts and Carlos Rodriguez. Coach Rodriguez later described his player's decision to marry like this: 'Psychologically, she needed to achieve something on her own. Her family had fallen apart and she needed to build something.'

Far from having fallen apart, the core of the Henin family was still as strong as it had always been. Justine's mother had passed away; but her father, sister and two brothers were all united, and her grandparents and uncles still loved her too. It was simply that Justine had turned her back on that very united family, choosing to recognise the existence of her aunts only.

It was interesting to hear Carlos admit that he had encouraged the wedding, even though he accepted that 'everybody was against her marriage'. Carlos explained: 'It was highly important to know the context. If 10 people ask me for advice, I won't tell them to marry, except for her in that very moment.' It was almost as though Rodriguez had become Justine's father. Almost, but not quite. 'It's as if (I am) but I'm not,' he explained. 'I'm harsh towards her. She tells me: "What I like about you is that you have no diplomacy, but you make yourself very clear."'

There was little diplomacy towards Justine's real family on her wedding day. With the support of Carlos keeping her strong, she wanted to marry with the people she chose to have around her, not those who might have expected to be there. And once the wedding was over, Rodriguez planned to push Justine out of her comfort zone on the tier just below the pinnacle of women's tennis, and make her prove to everyone, at last, that she was the best.

CHAPTER 13
THE WEDDING

ON 16 NOVEMBER 2002, JUSTINE WAS PREPARING TO become Henin-Hardenne. She was about to marry her sweetheart of four years, in twin ceremonies at the town hall in Marche-en-Famenne and the church of St Isidore, just a few hundred metres up the street from their first home in Marloie. For Jose Henin, the day was to be even more humiliating than he had allowed himself to expect. Among Justine's blood relatives in the Henin family, only Jose's sisters, Genevieve and Francoise, escaped the axe. They were invited to the ceremonies and subsequent reception at the 15th-century chateau of Lavaux-Sainte-Anne, a reward for the support that they had shown her during the feud.

That support continued on the big day itself, despite Justine's harsh treatment of the rest of their family. Not only was Jose to be denied the right to lead his daughter down the aisle, but Justine's siblings, Sarah, Thomas and David were similarly excluded. Neither her paternal uncles, Jean-Marie and Jean-Paul, received an invitation. Even her grandparents, Alphonse and Jeanne, were overlooked.

To make their pain bearable on the big day, Jose and the rest of his family congregated for a consolation meal in the Taverne du Centre, his brother Jean-Paul's friendly restaurant in the centre of Han-sur-Lesse. As Jose explained: 'We wanted to be together at this time. It would have been even worse to be alone as we contemplated what was to happen without us that day.' A major complication lay in the fact that Justine was only a short distance away from those she had cut off. She had chosen Genevieve's house, also in central Han-sur-Lesse, for her wedding preparations. It was almost as though she was oblivious to the added pain this would cause her closest relations.

The police force from the nearby town of Rochefort had become involved in security for the big occasion, even in little Han-sur-Lesse. Officers blocked one end of the street where, in the privacy of Genevieve's home, Justine had now slipped into her stylish wedding dress. Another two policemen were positioned at the other end of the same street to keep out any undesirables. Jose noted the police presence and wondered whether such measures were really necessary, since he couldn't see a single fan – obsessive or otherwise – loitering in the village to offer best wishes to his daughter on her special day. As it turned out, big crowds had gathered in Rochefort, through which the procession was due to pass later on; but from where Jose was sitting, the show of force in Han-sur-Lesse looked over the top, to say the least.

Before the day was very old, Jose became aware of a strange sensation. He explained later: 'I had this funny feeling that I was being watched or followed. I told my sons, Thomas and David. They laughed and told me I was really starting to lose it if I was getting that paranoid.'

Trying to shrug off this bizarre state of mind, Jose asked David to drive him down the rue de Grottes, the main shopping street in the village. Alphonse and Jeanne were waiting to be picked up from the quiet residential area at the end of the road, so they could be part of the rejected family's sombre gathering at the very least. Son and grandson picked up the elderly couple and began the short journey back to the restaurant. At precisely that moment, Sarah Henin was walking along the same street on her way to the restaurant for the family get-together. Suddenly, she heard the crackle of a walkie-talkie as one policeman tried to communicate with another. She distinctly heard the words: 'The car is on its way back towards the centre of the village.' She listened as he confirmed a number plate. It was her brother David's – she recognised it immediately. As soon as she was reunited with David and her father, she told them about her strange experience. Horrified but trying to stay calm, David confronted one of the policemen, a man he knew socially.

'Are we under surveillance?' he asked the officer-acquaintance.

'No,' came the embarrassed reply.

But David, a determined character, was in no mood to let the matter rest. 'My sister just heard you give out my number plate on your radio.'

That revelation made it difficult for the policeman to persist with his denials. He admitted that the authorities were keeping an eye on the uninvited section of the Henin family, just to make sure there was no possibility of an incident. Hearing this, Jose confronted the police officer in charge of the increasingly bizarre operation in Han-sur-Lesse, asking: 'Do you think this is really necessary?'

The police officer replied: 'We're just trying to make sure there isn't any trouble.'

'What kind of trouble?' Jose demanded.

The policeman looked him in the eye. 'We all know what happened to Monica Seles in Germany, don't we?'

Jose could scarcely believe what he was hearing. He recalled later: 'That was just a ridiculous thing to say. Seles was stabbed in the back by a crazy fan during a match against Steffi Graf. What did that have to do with my daughter's wedding?'

So he met the policeman's gaze and asked him straight out: 'Are you saying that you think I am capable of stabbing my daughter on her wedding day? Because if you are, you are the one who is crazy.'

When he got no response, Jose turned away in disgust and joined the rest of his loyal family in the restaurant, wondering who could have put the police up to their strange day's work.

A few minutes later, Justine's white limousine drove down the road on its way to the town hall in Marche-en-Famenne, where the first part of the ceremony, the signing of the paperwork, would take place in the presence of the mayor.

Meanwhile Jeanne, Justine's grandmother, had set her sights on reaching the venue for the service itself, the church of St Isidore in Marloie. The setting didn't exactly ooze romance. The church was a modern building, along with most of those in the village. A British aircraft had swooped in 1944 and knocked out a German munitions dump at the nearby station. When the munitions exploded, 10 Nazis, 40 locals and half the village buildings were taken with it. Scores of local people were mutilated and hundreds were injured. So modern Marloie was hardly the most beautiful place for a star bride to tie the knot with her young husband. Not that Jeanne could be deterred from going there for Justine's big day. She told me: 'I wanted to see her get married. I wanted at least to have that image to treasure in my head later. I didn't want to miss it.'

Her son Jean-Paul took up the story: 'My mother hadn't received an invitation to the church but she wanted me to take her there anyway. I explained that there was a fair chance we would be turned away, but still she insisted that we give it a try. My father, Alphonse, hadn't been feeling too well, so it was just the two of us.' Alphonse admitted to me later: 'I didn't want to cause a scandal.'

Jean-Paul continued: 'When we got to about 300 metres from the church, we came up against a police roadblock. I thought that might be it, but they let us through, even though they must have had details of the number plates of cars belonging to those members of the Henin family who hadn't been invited. So we arrived at the church, to astonished expressions on the faces of some of those who hadn't been expecting us. But I knew some of the security staff there, and they knew better than to turn away a 77-year-old woman, particularly when she was the grand-mother of the bride.

'We sat down in the church and my mother was so happy because she had a seat right by the aisle. It was towards the back, but she would still be able to see everything. The main thing was that Justine would pass right by on her way out with her new husband, and at the very least my mother would enjoy some eye contact with her granddaughter and perhaps they would be able to give each other a nod or a smile.'

Justine entered in a beautiful ivory dress, a perfect blend of classic and modern styles. She was led to the altar by her uncle, Hugues Bastin, the husband of her aunt Francoise. Bastin wasn't even her flesh and blood, and Jean-Paul knew it should have been his brother up there, giving away his daughter in the traditional manner. To rub further salt into Jose's wounds, Carlos Rodriguez, sat in a place of honour among her guests.

The ceremony went smoothly, Justine holding a huge bouquet of white roses and Pierre-Yves looking dapper in tailed jacket, waistcoat and striped trousers. It was not long before the time had come for the newly wedded couple to kiss and make their way back down the aisle, returning the smiles of their loved ones as they went.

Jean-Paul recalled: 'Justine came up the aisle towards us with Pierre-Yves. Now she was right next to her grand-mother, whose white hair is unmistakable, even in photographs of the day taken from behind the altar. My mother smiled at Justine and tried to get some eye contact with her.'

Jeanne's sense of disbelief was still evident when she took up the story: 'We were only about 50 centimetres apart, and she knew full well I was there. She knew I was looking at her. I felt it. And she just walked straight past.'

CHAPTER 14
BEYOND SPORT

THE SOFT RED CLAY OF THE COURT PHILIPPE CHATRIER, Roland Garros, was about to stage yet another titanic struggle. It was 5 June 2003, and Justine Henin-Hardenne was about to face Serena Williams in the semi-final of the French Open. She felt better equipped to confront the might of a Williams sister than ever before. During the winter, she had enlisted the help of a fitness coach with a fearsome reputation for putting his charges through torturous physical regimes. Pat Etcheberry had worked with Pete Sampras, Jim Courier and a host of other top players. He had spent December 2002 working Justine so hard that she was frequently close to tears. That didn't stop her doing as she was told. She came back with visible muscles.

Etcheberry and Carlos Rodriguez had worked on her mind too, and warned her that the time had come to take her self-belief to another level, because the alternative was to be regarded forever as an also-ran who didn't have a Grand Slam title in her. Rodriguez explained: 'I am a polite, pleasant man, but I can be a son-of-a-bitch if I feel it's necessary to provoke, in order to take Justine to the objective she herself has chosen.'

Justine reflected: 'Early in 2003 I felt something was different. I was number four, number five in the world at this time. I said to myself: "Do you want to stay at this ranking, or do you want to become a champion and win Grand Slams?" I had worked in Florida with Pat Etcheberry and mentally I changed a lot of things. I understood the efforts I had to make if I wanted to become a champion.'

And in the end it was Justine's choice, and no one else's, to proceed as she did. She was going to push new physical and psychological boundaries, even if it meant exploring the outer limits of what is acceptable in sport. Her attitude to Serena that day would reflect all the pain she had been through.

As a French speaker, Justine certainly had the Roland Garros fans on her side. Only a tiny minority of the 14,000 supporters gathered that day beneath a burning Parisian sky were Americans. High clouds softened the sunlight every so often, bringing relief to the crowd below. But such respite was only temporary, and there would be no escape from the heat or pressure for the gladiators below.

Dressed in a white cap, white top and grey skirt, Justine looked unremarkable as she marched out behind the favourite. In the bright afternoon glare her skin looked pale and blotchy. To anyone unaware of her fighting spirit, it seemed that the impressive surroundings and the sheer magnitude of the occasion might prove too much for her. Serena's outfit celebrated her love for innovative sports-wear design. One shoulder strap was pure silver glitz, the other orange, like her top. Her skirt was the same striking orange, and she oozed glamour and confidence. Even her footwear was orange and white, and although traditionalists might have considered the look to be excessively flashy, Serena's talent and strength as a relentless sporting warrior had helped her win 31 of her 33 matches so far that year. In short, she had earned the right to wear whatever she liked.

On this particular day, however, there were reasons why the French crowd were keen to see an end to that amazing record of victories, and not just because they treated Justine, their Belgian neighbour, as one of their own. First there was the political dimension. Serena was an American and, in some respects, she was in the wrong place at the wrong time. George W. Bush had recently condemned the French for their refusal to support his invasion of Iraq, and was encouraging a boycott of French goods across the Atlantic. America's last remaining representative at Roland Garros faced a possible backlash. Then there was the racial element, also hard to quantify. Was it possible that the crowd's hostility might prove to be more intense because Serena was black? The far right had enjoyed a shocking amount of political support in France, despite the many black sportsmen and women who had done the nation proud over the years. Prejudice is easier to express from the safety of a big group, although there is no proof that what followed was racially motivated.

One thing was certain: Serena Williams was walking into a cauldron, and the Portuguese umpire, Jorge Dias, would be hard-pressed to maintain order and dignity as the afternoon wore on. This would be about as brutal and confrontational as tennis ever got. With 25 wins in 27 matches in 2003, Justine Henin-Hardenne was no more likely to cave in under pressure than Serena. Indeed, the American saw her very first service game broken by a stunning backhand pass, Justine's trademark. The Belgian girl held her own serve with a disdainful forehand winner and already Rodriguez was nodding with satisfaction.

Henin-Hardenne didn't just break Serena's serve a second time, she achieved it without the taller woman winning so much as a point. The crowd went wild and the chant of 'JuJu, JuJu' could already be heard all around her. It was 3-0, a start beyond Justine's wildest dreams. With a series of smashes, Serena broke straight back and screamed loudly as she sent her opponent scrambling all over the court. At 3-2 Pierre-Yves was pictured with his head bowed, a young man clearly feeling the tension as much as his wife. To his relief, however, it was Serena's act that fell apart again, Justine winning her next service game to love. At deuce on Serena's serve, the women fought out a punishing 13-shot rally before Serena netted and Justine clenched her fist. Soon Henin-Hardenne was 5-2 ahead.

Justine's wonderful backhand gave her two set points in the very next game. Then, under immense pressure, Serena came up with a superhuman forehand pass, and even Pierre-Yves had to smile. When Justine only found the net on her next set point, the situation suddenly became more serious. Surprising power on her forehand gave Henin-Hardenne another chance to close out. And when it mattered, she came up with an ace to take the first set 6-2.

Pandemonium broke out all around Roland Garros. In half an hour, Justine had brought the world number one to her knees. And as the second set got under way, any line call that went against the crowd's favourite sparked howls of protest, any time Serena tried to stick up for herself, she was shouted down almost before she had started. The match was moving out of the realms of sport.

When Serena double-faulted in the next game, the crowd actually applauded. She grew angry, and stepped up a gear to win a series of bludgeoning rallies. Williams roared like a lioness as she went 3-2 ahead, and yelled an audible 'come on!' as she broke to take a 5-3 lead. Since no one, other than her mother Oracene, seemed to be supporting her, it was as if Serena had taken on the role of chief cheerleader for herself. But Justine fought like a tiger to break back at the end of a 16-stroke rally, and now it was 5-4. After the changeover Serena attacked her opponent's serve, and she did so with such controlled ferocity that pretty soon Justine was facing set point. She defended desperately, dashing from one corner to the other, until finally she could run no more and failed to clear the net. Serena had taken the second set 6-4, and ominously she didn't even bother to celebrate.

Justine's serve began to look increasingly wobbly in the final set, and her stroke-play was looking tired too. Serena allowed herself to show some joy when she broke to go 3-1 ahead, but Justine wasn't finished. From nowhere she conjured an amazing cross-court backhand under pressure, and Serena looked so surprised at her opponent's new burst of life that she failed to win a single point on her key service game. Justine was back in it at 3-2, and promptly shot herself in the foot by overcooking one shot after another to forfeit her own service with equal ease.

At 2-4 in the final set, Justine's long-held dreams were evaporating before her eyes, and Serena moved in for the kill. A 16-stroke rally reminded tennis lovers what a magnificent match these two had provided, and just how much talent there was to celebrate out on court. But Justine was first to fail, sending her backhand wide on the run. Serena clenched her fist and screamed as she sensed that another key moment had gone her way. In contrast, Justine allowed her head to drop as she shut her eyes, perhaps in prayer.

They squared up again with a new series of pulverising blows; but Justine's accuracy under pressure deserted her again and a forehand flew fractionally long. This set in motion a chain of events that was to give the semi-final a controversial place in tennis history. Even though Serena clearly gestured to her opponent that the ball was out, pointing to the mark with her racket, Justine walked over to umpire Dias and exercised her right to request that he examine for himself the spot where the ball had landed. Dutifully, he stepped down from the chair and walked towards the end where Serena was waiting. The American advanced slightly, quite willing to show him the mark, but he motioned for her to keep her distance while he conducted an independent investigation. Serena threw her arms out in despair, as if insufficient respect had been shown for her own sporting reputation. In an instant, Dias backed Serena's original claim and returned to the chair. Serena shook her head, obviously hurt that her word had been so blatantly questioned.

When Dias announced the score to be 30-0, the crowd erupted in fury yet again, their whistles and jeers an indication of Justine's perilous predicament. At 4-2 and 30-0, it was almost all over. Widespread dissent could still be heard as Justine crouched down in readiness to receive. Blanking out the wall of noise, Serena threw the ball up to take her next serve. At that precise moment Justine raised her left hand, and the Williams serve dipped into the net. Now the jeers turned to cheers at the American's failure, and no one seemed keen to acknowledge the fact that Serena might have been distracted by Henin-Hardenne's belated gesture. All the umpire did was to say: 'S'il vous plaît' [Please] in a bid to silence the rowdy crowd.

Serena raised a ball in the direction of Dias and said: 'First serve.'

Dias looked confused.

'First serve,' a dumbfounded Serena repeated. 'First serve.'

'What?' The umpire didn't understand why.

'She had her hand up,' Serena explained patiently, glancing across at Justine for verification. 'She had her hand up,' repeated the American, her glance at Henin-Hardenne turning into a glare the moment she realised no such confirmation was going to come.

'I didn't see that,' Dias admitted, glancing at both sides of the net.

'What?' Serena's expression suggested that she could hardly believe what was happening. She looked at a poker-faced Justine with what appeared to be a mounting sense of outrage at her failure to come clean. Yet there was something more than anger written in her expression – hurt. Was it because a fellow warrior had seemed to show so little honour in battle, and perhaps allowed her hunger for the prize to obscure what sport was supposed to be all about?

Had the score not been so overwhelmingly in her favour, perhaps Serena would have worked harder to force a confession out of her opponent. But such a move would also have caused anarchy in the stands, and maybe she had allowed herself to be intimidated by the abuse she had received every time she tried to fight her corner. Justine continued to wait for the second serve, like a trapped animal suddenly shown an escape route. It was the turning point.

CHAPTER 15
WINNING DIRTY, TALKING CLEAN

AS JUSTINE HENIN-HARDENNE LATCHED ONTO THAT spinning Serena second serve and took control of the point, there was no sign of guilt for any part she might have played in the confusion. Williams began to struggle to clear the net with her shots, and every time she served up a fault the crowd cheered gleefully. This wasn't tennis, it was more like sadism. 'S'il vous plaît,' was all the feeble umpire could say. He had lost control, and so had Serena. With a superb forehand winner, Justine finished the game. She had broken back at 3-4, and a truly awesome backhand brought the games level. The fans greeted a double-fault by Serena with deafening cheers during her next service, and pretty soon Justine was serving for the match at 5-4. Two double-faults and two unforced errors later, Henin-Hardenne had choked and it was all square at 5-5.

The gritty Belgian girl regained her composure and fought her way to break point. Disgracefully, the American was forced to hesitate on her next, vital serve due to more unsporting noise from the crowd. When she was finally able to continue, Justine returned with relish and produced a series of wounding blows that forced Serena into her own fatal error. It was 6-5 and chaos broke out around the court Philippe Chatrier. Henin-Hardenne had earned herself the right to serve for the match yet again.

During the interval, Justine stopped hiding her head under her towel and glanced up at Carlos. He shot her an emphatic nod, seeming to invite no further visual dialogue. He was telling her that enough was enough – he wanted it to be over. Shortly afterwards Justine had three match points, Williams' resistance finally weakening. A crescendo of screams and shouts forced Henin-Hardenne to hesitate as she prepared to deliver the killer thrust. The serve went wide. More delays preceded her second effort, which finally arrowed over the net with lethal force. Serena's backhand return landed out and the public execution of a proud champion was over. The will of the baying mob had been done, and sport was almost forgotten.

Justine pumped her arms in the air, having achieved her aim. In the box, Pierre-Yves hugged Carlos, and then looked down lovingly at the winner. If the fight, streaked with flashes of sublime tennis, hadn't turned so very ugly towards the end, their moment of triumph would have been touching.

Serena forced herself to accept Justine's cursory handshake and prepared to leave the arena. She heard herself jeered loudly by the merciless Roland Garros crowd. Williams had forgotten to shake the umpire's hand, and now she was being cast as the villain of the piece. Maintaining her dignity to the last, she went back to Jorge Dias and made amends. As Serena finally left the scene of her nightmare she waved, only to be greeted with more jeers. At least the spectators were consistent.

Justine was asked about the crowd in her press conference less than an hour later. 'I think the crowd gave me all the support I needed to win the match,' she said cheerfully. 'It was unbelievable playing in this atmosphere. So I was happy they were totally behind me . . .'

'Was it a fair crowd?' The question seemed to stun Henin-Hardenne. 'Was it a fair crowd? Don't you think it was a little bit too much against Serena?'

'Yeah,' she acknowledged at last, 'sometimes it could be a little bit too much. It's true that when she was missing first serves, yeah, they were . . . But you know, that's tennis. It's like this. I think they wanted so much that I won this match, so I understand them. And so I say thank you to them, but it's true that sometimes it was a little bit too much.'

She had been rather more critical of unruly crowd behaviour during her Federation Cup campaign in Madrid in November 2001, though as the victim in Spain that was perhaps natural.

Later in her press conference Justine was asked if Serena had said anything to her at the end of the match.

'No,' she admitted.

But Serena said plenty when it was her turn to face the media. 'It was a tough crowd out there today, really. Very tough – story of my life.' When asked to explain that last remark, she burst into tears. And when pushed on Justine's hand gesture, the one that had cost Serena a first serve when she was closing in on victory, the American's attempt at diplomacy soon crumbled. 'Well, I mean, obviously I'm not upset with her. Actually, OK, I was a little disappointed with her because . . . you know, it wasn't the turning point of the match. But to start lying and fabricating, it's not fair. I understand that, you know, people want to win these days, but . . . I don't know.'

In her own post-match interview, Justine had insisted that she understood the greater importance of life beyond sport. She explained: 'It's fantastic to beat Serena in the French Open, but there are many other important things in life . . . The day when I got married was the nicest day of my life. I cannot compare that to a victory like today. So you have to put things in perspective. Tennis is a beautiful sport. It's fantastic when you can win, especially with this type of ambience, but you must realise that there are things in life that are much more important.'

Especially with this type of ambience? Serena begged to differ. 'I think it's bad when people start booing in between serves, you know, or other people are egging them on by doing ridiculous things. So that gets a little tough, you know.'

She was asked: 'Did it get worse when you questioned a couple of calls?'

'I didn't question any calls,' she pointed out.

'The umpire, the chair came down?'

'The balls were clearly out,' she stated.

'It seemed to get worse after that,' the journalist maintained.

And Serena took the bait. 'Yeah, for some reason . . . I don't know. Like, you know, when a player circles a ball, I can see that it's out. I don't necessarily call the umpire and say, "Go check it." The point is not going to change the match.' Then, remembering to maintain her dignity, she added: 'Like I said, she played very well today and she probably deserved to win. She was the better player today, really.'

But those two points at 4-2 had changed the match, whatever the players said afterwards. Deep down Serena must have known it, and surely Justine knew it too. Psychologically, she was now every bit as tough as her coach and her husband wanted her to be. She hinted at this in a revealing post-match remark: 'Winning matches like this means I'm starting to believe that one day I could be at the top, really at the top. And I'm playing good right now, you know. It's sometimes very difficult to explain why I'm doing better. But I was able to make the right decisions and I have good people around me, and I'm feeling good in my private life, so it's helping me to be 100 per cent on the court.'

Back in Belgium, Jose had watched his daughter's match on television. He wasn't entirely proud of Justine's conduct, and said: 'If Serena had served an ace while Justine had her hand up, I suspect my daughter would have confessed to putting her hand up. In my opinion she was wrong in what she did. But maybe that's why she won. If she had given Serena two serves, as she should have done, imagine if Serena had served an ace. It would have been 4-2 and 40-0 in the third set. That would have changed a lot of things. But she did it and so she at least has to explain herself.'

Deep down, however, Jose understood only too well why his daughter had allowed herself to behave as she did that day, why she harboured such an obsessive desire for victory at Roland Garros. For nothing explained Justine better than her own past and nothing sharpened her hunger for French Open glory quite like a promise she had made to her mother, all those years ago.

CHAPTER 16
FLORENCE AND THE FOOTBALL MATCH

JUSTINE HENIN IS JOSE'S ELDER DAUGHTER, BUT NOT HIS first. Florence Henin will always be Justine's big sister, even though she didn't reach much of an age. What happened to Florence, more than 30 years ago, started a chain of emotional reactions that may have led to the chaos within the Henin family at the start of the 21st century. And as she ruthlessly set about conquering the world of tennis, perhaps even Justine didn't know the full story, or appreciate the long-term consequences of a tragedy that took place before she was born.

At two and a half, Florence was already desperate to be older. It was as though she wanted to reach the next stage of her childhood as fast as she could. Jose, her proud father, often took her on walks down the rue de Grottes – in their home village of Han-sur-Lesse. He recalled: 'Florence used to love watching the other children, some as young as three, on their way to the nursery school behind the village church. She used to look up at me through her blonde hair and say: "Papa, I want to go too! Let me go to school with the other children." I'd smile down at her and reply: "Not long now, darling, just a few months more and you'll be old enough." It wasn't just the other children she loved. Florence adored old people and used to spend much of her time with her great-grandmothers, who both lived near the stream and the famous caves at the bottom of the village.'

One great-grandmother was called Julienne, and she lived in a house right opposite Jose's parents, Alphonse and Jeanne. The other great-grandmother, Marie, was bedridden, so Alphonse and Jeanne gave her a room in their home. That way she too could be close to her loved ones. Life was still special for Marie because Florence adored her so much. It wasn't unusual for the little girl to visit her 10 or 12 times a day, to tell her what she had been doing and ask the frail old woman how she was feeling.

Florence was also very close to her maternal grandfather, Georges Rosiere, and they would often be seen walking through the village together. Feeling secure under this protective family umbrella, Florence became the friendliest child imaginable. Jose remembered: 'She was hardly ever any trouble and seemed to cry a lot less than the other children we knew.' She seemed to sleep less, too. Her grandmother Jeanne recalled: 'It was as though she knew time was short and wanted to make the most of every waking hour.' Alphonse added: 'And how she could talk! At just two years old, she spoke like a lawyer. I've never heard anything like it, before or since.'

Jose's wife, Francoise, fell pregnant again towards the end of January 1973; both parents were delighted with their timing. Jose explained: 'Apart from anything, we were thrilled for Florence, because we thought she would soon have a little brother or sister for company. We knew she had all the qualities to fulfil the role of big sister to perfection, since she had already developed this caring, considerate side to her nature. It seemed to come from somewhere well beyond her years.'

But no child is perfect, and Florence wasn't old enough to have worked out why it might not always be a good idea to burst into her parents' bedroom early in the morning and climb into bed with them. When she bounced onto the parental pillows early one Saturday morning in May 1973, two factors prompted her mother to reproach her. First, she was four months pregnant by then and valued her sleep. Second, Jose was due to play in one of the most important football matches of his life that afternoon, and his wife knew that he, too, would appreciate a lie-in before his big challenge. So Francoise frowned at her daughter and said: 'Florence, this is the last time we let you do this. Mummy and Daddy need to be peaceful together sometimes.' Jose recalled: 'She gave us such a smile that we let her stay in bed with us anyway. But she knew it would be the last time.'

By now Jose's mind had already turned to football. It was a game he had always loved and taken seriously. Standard Liege, one of the most famous clubs in Belgium, had shown an interest in Jose's progress when he was younger. But somehow he had never wanted to make the many sacrifices necessary to try to break into professional football. He was still a very useful striker though, and played for his local team, Han-sur-Lesse. The end-of-season play-off against nearby Neffe was only hours away. The prize for the winner would be promotion to Division Two of the Namur District League. It might not have been a sporting contest of national importance, but you couldn't tell that to anyone in the village above the caves. To them, it was a matter of life and death.

Jose shouldn't really have played, since he had broken his wrist only two weeks earlier. But he hated the idea of missing the big match, especially when 700 local people were expected to cheer on their heroes. Call it ego or a keen sense of responsibility to the team, but Jose decided to take off his plaster early and play his part.

This was very much a family affair. Apart from Jose, his younger brother Jean-Marie operated just behind the front two, while his other brother Jean-Paul acted as the team's sweeper and hatchet man in defence. If any opposition player dared to foul one of his brothers with a degree of violent intent, Jean-Paul would walk up to the offender quite casually and say: 'You have less than five minutes left on this pitch.' More often than not, Jean-Paul found a way to keep his word with a bone-crunching revenge tackle, one that soon forced his target to limp off in agony – if indeed he didn't need to be carried.

That May, the Henin brothers were already the toast of the village because they had enjoyed such an exceptional season. However, each man knew that his good work would count for nothing if the team didn't win on that final, fateful day.

After a light lunch, Jose said goodbye to Francoise and Florence. Both ladies were fragile in different ways, one pregnant and the other tiny, so mother and daughter had decided to avoid the chaos at the football ground and settle instead for the peace of the village playground.

The Han-sur-Lesse football ground boasted an impressive modern stand running along one side of the pitch, and there was even a set of working floodlights at the club's disposal. You could hardly call it a glamorous stadium, with the village cemetery rolling up a gentle slope above one touchline. But on this particular day the humble arena could have been Barcelona's Nou Camp or Milan's San Siro, such was the sense of anticipation and excitement. The adrenalin pumped through the Henin blood as each brother changed into his familiar white strip and prepared for battle.

With hundreds of screaming supporters turning up the heat, the players were so nervous that they felt considerable relief when the match finally kicked off. Under such extreme pressure, Han-sur-Lesse didn't achieve the domination they had expected. Even the starring trio of Henin brothers struggled to find their best form on the day. After 85 minutes, the scores were locked at one-all and the home side was lucky to be on level terms. That's when a player called Michel Delculee, who had only just joined the Han-sur-Lesse team, set in motion a chain of events that would lead to disaster. Timing his run to perfection, he met a cross with incredible force and his header flew into the top corner of the net from outside the area.

The crowd erupted, there was pandemonium all around the pitch, and the shell-shocked Neffe team didn't have time to hit back. The final whistle blew, Han-sur-Lesse was promoted and wild celebrations began in earnest. Tragically, they were heading in Florence Henin's direction.

With horns sounding and pedestrians dancing, a spontaneous procession passed through the centre of the village and headed down the rue de Grottes, towards the house where the Henin brothers' parents lived. One wag had decided that their mother, Jeanne, should be presented with flowers, since she, above all, could be considered responsible for the team's promotion. After all, Jeanne had brought the three best Han-sur-Lesse players into the world, and therefore it was only logical that she should be hailed as the true heroine of the hour!

Her sons were thrust to the head of the procession and witnessed the touching presentation of a bouquet to their blushing, speechless mother. Out of the corner of his eye, Jose noticed that Francoise and their daughter were already back from the park. Usually Florence would have played there until late into the evening, laughing and skipping with her friends as they enjoyed the lingering light of early summer. Jose remembered: 'My wife simply told me she had decided to bring Florence home early, she didn't know why. Perhaps they wanted to hear how the match had been won.'

Florence stood beside the gate to the small front garden at her grandparents' home. Her great-grandmother Julienne was right next to her as the procession of cars ground to a halt. Since Alphonse and Jeanne lived in one of the last houses on the rue de Grottes, and a stream made the street a dead end there, the cars began to execute three-point turns. Still hooting and waving, most of the drivers achieved their aim with ease. There was one exception.

Jose recalled: 'I stood in conversation with a friend, soaking up the glory, just a few metres from my daughter and grandmother. Suddenly a yellow Toyota jolted and flew at the gate with a terrible roar. Before she even had time to scream, Florence was dragged under the car. Julienne was also hit and thrown high into the air. She crashed against the wall of the house before landing in a heap outside the front door. For a second I froze in horror as the car, with Florence trapped below, shuddered to a violent halt in the garden.'

CHAPTER 17
THE LEGACY

WHAT JOSE HAD WITNESSED WITH HIS OWN EYES WAS SO unspeakably horrible that for a few moments he simply couldn't take it in. He remembered: 'Friends immediately dived beneath the Toyota and pulled Florence out. She wasn't moving and we carried her into the house to try to revive her. Others tended to Julienne, who was conscious and in terrible pain.

'I looked at my daughter, who was lifeless but strangely unscathed. It seemed so bizarre that there wasn't a mark on her body. How could she be dead when she still looked so beautiful? I couldn't face this awful sight for a moment longer and staggered into the back garden in a deep state of shock. Perhaps I should have tended to my wife, Francoise, who was distraught, but I just couldn't. I was numb and shaking, beside myself with grief. I just stood there, trying to take in the horror of what had happened.'

Jose knew the young man who had caused the tragedy. Later, it emerged that the offender had been drinking and didn't own a driving licence. The culprit was the younger brother of another player in the Han-sur-Lesse football team. Jose didn't know how he was going to make him pay for what he had done, but any thoughts of retribution were suddenly disturbed by the sound of shouting from inside the house.

'Jose, she's alive! Florence has woken up! She seems to be OK!'

Scarcely daring to believe his ears, Jose ran back into the house and saw his daughter looking up at him, fully conscious but a little bemused. 'I'm thirsty,' is all she said. 'I'm very thirsty.'

Her father felt that he had witnessed a miracle and there were tears of relief when the doctor-on-call arrived to confirm what Jose and Francoise had prayed for. It seemed they had been spared every parent's worst nightmare. 'I can't see any signs of lasting damage,' the doctor said, adding, almost as an afterthought. 'Better get her to hospital though, just to make sure.'

Although the ambulance had already been called, it took half an hour to arrive. Jose and Francoise climbed in to accompany their daughter on the 20-minute journey to the nearest hospital in Marche. There, doctors studied Florence's eyes more carefully, and saw something that seemed to cause them deep concern. 'She will have to go to hospital in Liege,' they announced quickly. 'There's no time to waste.'

Within 10 minutes the confused child, who had complained only of excessive thirst, was dispatched to the big city with more sirens wailing, her anxious parents still by her side. Their only comfort lay in the fact that Florence showed precious few signs of distress, and they knew she would soon have the very best experts and equipment to help her.

Jose took up the story. 'On that hour-long journey, she quietly began to slip away. We still didn't understand, because she had survived the impact without a scratch. We thought the worst was over. We saw her close her eyes and thought perhaps she was just sleepy now. But the frantic reactions of the medical staff soon told us a different story. By the time we reached that hospital in Liege, Florence was dead.'

It transpired that the crushing impact with the car had ruptured her liver, which had then burst inside her body. She had suffered massive internal bleeding and the autopsy showed that no one on earth could have saved her. She was still only two and a half.

Jose recalled the moment when all hope was taken away: 'When we were told in Liege that she was gone forever, we didn't know what to believe or how to react. She had been taken from us, given back in one piece as if by a miracle, then taken away again – all in the space of two hours. It seemed too ridiculous to be true – some kind of grotesque joke. Three hours earlier, I'd been worried about the result of a football match, which had seemed to me then like a matter of life and death. Now we knew what it really was to face such a moment – and it wouldn't be the last time.'

Julienne had somehow survived the impact of car and wall. The elderly woman had sustained shattered hips and gone into severe shock. She spent four months in hospital, but she pulled through and returned home fully recovered. Florence's other great-grandmother, bedridden throughout the commotion on that dreadful Saturday, didn't fare so well. Marie waited in vain for further visits from Florence, whose body was released after two days and brought back to the very same house. As family and friends paid their respects downstairs, no one dared to tell Marie what had happened. She never asked about her great-granddaughter and perhaps she didn't need to. The expressions on the faces of those who visited her room probably told the story better than words ever could. She didn't know that Florence had died on 6 May. However, already a frail woman, Marie died on 23 May. Some of the Henin family think she wanted to go and look after her favourite little girl.

Still four months pregnant, Francoise could have been forgiven for wondering what she had done to deserve so much trauma. At 14, she had tried to face the devastation of losing her mother, Bearthe, to cancer. Now she had lost her daughter. It was more than any pregnant woman could be expected to take. Overnight, much of her mousy-brown hair turned grey. But somehow she struggled on, to protect the baby inside her. It is a tribute to her selfless determination that she also decided to visit Julienne in hospital just a week after the tragedy. The lingering shock and extra weight that Francoise now carried combined to make her legs unsteady. As she climbed the hospital steps to see Julienne that day, she slipped and broke her foot. Bereaved and prematurely grey, Francoise now had a new problem – how to cope with pregnancy on crutches. Undaunted, however, she eventually gave birth to a son, David.

Jose recalled: 'It came as no surprise to us when he showed initial signs of having a nervous nature as a toddler. They say any trauma that a pregnant woman suffers, her baby also feels in her womb. Personally, I can well believe it.'

He also believed that Florence's death, and what happened in the days that followed, might have planted more than just a sense of despair in the body of his wife. He speculated: 'Some experts say that cancer can lie dormant for decades. If stress really can cause it, then perhaps my wife's eventual destiny was also decided that month.'

The drunk driver who killed Florence was released from prison after little more than a month. He even returned to the area, leaving Jose to fight the impulse for revenge. He revealed: 'When the driver showed his face around the village in the following months, I ignored him and he ignored me. I don't think he really knew what he could say. "Sorry" wasn't going to bring Florence back, after all. I tried to leave my anger behind, and eventually I succeeded, because I knew the boy didn't mean to kill my daughter. Yes, he had been drinking and he didn't have a licence. But he didn't set out that day to ruin my family. It was an accident. I don't even want to make him suffer by naming him here.'

Justine knows enough about what happened all those years ago to understand that sporting success is not in itself the key to life. But she has also learned how fragile life can be, and the need to seize the day is ingrained in her character. As she grew up, the memory of her sister was never very far away, whether she liked it or not. Jose explained: 'Justine was brought up to remember her big sister's loving character and how cruelly her life was cut short. We tried to make it so that she knew Florence almost as a living person. I have passed on that same knowledge to her brothers, David and Thomas, and her little sister, Sarah.

'My wife Francoise and I decided that it was right to preserve the memory of Florence so vividly for them. But I have never tried to set her memory above my love and respect for my other children in any way whatsoever. I have merely offered them some intimate knowledge of a wonderful sister, a little girl they were sadly unable to meet personally.

'Not a day goes by when I don't think of Florence. It may be for five seconds or 10 minutes, but I remember her. Regrets can last a lifetime. They play on your mind. My decision to take off that wrist plaster back in 1973 and play the match . . . That ridiculous header, the one that won us the game so undeservedly, and sparked the celebration in my village . . . And my wife, how do you think she felt? When she told Florence off that Saturday morning, she didn't know it would be the last time our daughter would ever be able to get into bed with us. When they came back from the park earlier than usual that afternoon, how were they to know what would happen? We all had to live with the consequences of our actions, and we tried to forgive others and ourselves. What happened caused all sorts of regrets and stayed in our marriage for a long time afterwards. But I feel happy that the brothers and sisters who came into the world after her may also think about her and even love her if they wish to do so in their own private way.'

Florence's short life and cruel death may well have had a psychological impact on Justine. It may not be exaggerating the case to suggest that she has been competing against a ghost all her life, the perfect image of an elder sister long departed. No wonder the middle Henin sister, Justine, developed an almost obsessive desire to distinguish herself in everything she did, and pursued her tennis talent, from the moment she discovered it, with an intensity that would make her the world's number one player.

The impact of Florence's death on Jose may have had even more obvious repercussions for the young tennis star. He said: 'I certainly don't offer what happened to Florence as some kind of excuse for any errors of judgement of which I may have been guilty when it came to Justine. But sometimes I wonder if my overanxious behaviour had its root in the fear of losing another daughter.

'It was years before Francoise and I felt ready to have another baby girl. We were relieved when our next two children were sons. By the time Justine came along, we thought we were ready for another daughter and we were delighted. But perhaps there was still an underlying fear of losing her. Maybe that fear caused the sort of suffocating love that Justine talks about, the kind she claims drove her away. Perhaps I was overprotective or interfering at times. I was certainly not a perfect father. I have made errors of judgement like any normal person and I am sorry for those.'

CHAPTER 18
A PROMISE TO MUM

AFTER TWO BABY BOYS, DAVID AND THOMAS, JUSTINE arrived on 1 June 1982. She was born in Liege, where Florence had been heading when she succumbed to her injuries in 1973, and where David's life would be saved all those years later in 2007.

Although Florence was never far from her parents' thoughts during Justine's early years, Francoise and Jose quickly saw that their latest daughter was a bubbly individual in her own right, unique and distinct from the little girl they had lost. Perhaps she was less tactile, maybe more of a tomboy, but she was still a sheer delight. Like Florence, she seemed to have an extraordinary force of personality for someone so young. As she passed the age at which Florence had been so cruelly taken away, Francoise and Jose realised that their small and deceptively robust second daughter was starting to show an appetite for sport. By the time her little sister, Sarah, came into the world, Justine was five and already mixing it with the local boys on the football field. She wore her hair short and straight like the opposition.

Justine recalled: 'My brothers were playing football and tennis and I followed them, so I was with boys all the time. I started in a boys' football team and I scored eight goals in one match. One of the boys on the other team was crying and his parents were saying: "It doesn't matter." And he was saying: "Yeah, but it's a girl!" That was really funny.'

Someone with Justine's fiercely competitive streak was hardly going to start firing wide just because some poor boy couldn't handle losing to a girl. She carried on playing football right through to the age of 12 and continued to score more goals than anyone else. At five, however, a new passion had emerged – one that would eclipse her love for football or anything else. Jose later explained how an incredible sporting story started. 'I was playing a tennis match at a small tournament in Nassogne, not far from home,' he recalled. 'Justine had picked up the scoring system and she was shouting the points for the crowd. "It's 4-2 and 15-0," she would tell everyone. People didn't mind, because she was right. Even if my wife, Francoise, went off to get a drink, she knew Justine would update her correctly when she got back.'

'After the match, Justine said: "Papa! I want to play!" So there she was, aged five, and she had hold of this huge racket. We started to play and people were amazed. She played so well! She saw the ball beautifully. She attacked it when she needed to and stepped back at the right time to make space, too. A member of the Nassogne club took me aside and told me: "I think you need to get her a good teacher. She can be big." I smiled.'

Before Jose and Francoise took that step, they waited to see whether Justine would develop an appetite for tennis comparable to her love of football. Sure enough, every time

Jose played, Justine would step onto the court for five minutes afterwards, enthusiastically developing her skills and range of shots.

Her parents were amazed by what happened next, although it did at least mean that Francoise would have plenty of time to look after her toddler, Sarah, without needing to worry too much about how to keep Justine occupied and happy.

Jose recalled: 'That Christmas, 1987, we bought Justine a little tennis racket. She was five but through that winter she played thousands of volleys against the kitchen wall.' When the warmer weather arrived she wasn't slow to take advantage, and Jose added: 'We took her down to the local tennis club in Rochefort. She played all day. She would start at 9.00am, and only break for lunch at midday. By 1.30pm she was back on the tennis courts. And that is where she would stay, until 7.00pm or 8.00pm if she could. Francoise and I would go down and watch her, and eventually in the evening we would take her home. The only question was whether she had played six, seven or eight hours of tennis on any given day.'

Justine told everyone who would listen that one day she would be the best in the world. Her mother heard this boast more often than most, and Jose still remembered her reaction fondly as she looked back in 2004. 'My wife would smile and tell Justine she was right. She would be the best in the world. Not everyone she told was so sure, and it is incredible to think that it all came true.'

Justine already seemed prepared to work harder than anyone else and make more sacrifices to make her dream a reality. Jose explained: 'After a while, the director of the Rochefort club delicately pointed out that Justine's new passion had given rise to a minor problem: other members couldn't get on court! But Justine was certainly in demand among the other youngsters. All the kids, even up to 10 and 11, came calling for Justine at home if she wasn't at the club. They wanted to face the incredible six-year-old and see if they could learn something!'

When the local kids could no longer provide stiff enough opposition to give Justine a proper game, she began to test her skills against Jose and Thomas. But her father soon went to the Belgian Tennis Federation, who had adopted a new type of game for youngsters called mini-tennis. And by the time Justine was six-and-a-half, she was practising in a more professional environment at the Saint Gilles club in Ciney under a coach called Patrick Sacre. 'This was when Justine really discovered that fantastic backhand action, using only one hand,' said Jose. 'She didn't need two hands because the shot flowed so naturally with one. In fact, she played stronger single-handed backhands than older girls could manage with two!'

Nick Bollettieri, the USA's foremost coaching guru, spotted the shot that would become Justine's trademark at a coaching clinic he held for hundreds of hopefuls one day in Brussels. 'What was that?!' asked an astonished Bollettieri when she unleashed a bullet of a backhand straight back over the net for a winner. He sought out Jose and didn't waste words. 'I want to work with her. I want her with me now, in Florida.' This led to several visits over the years to Bollettieri's coaching school in Bradenton, Florida, although Justine always made it clear that she wasn't prepared to spend any great length of time away from her family.

In 1992 Justine took an Under 10s title in Brussels and won two tickets to Roland Garros to see her favourite player, Steffi Graf, take on the hottest new talent in the game, Monica Seles, in the French Open final. Roland Garros was a sacred venue for French-speaking players, bigger than Wimbledon, and the prize was like a dream. A resourceful Jose found two extra tickets to a different part of the arena. So it was decided that Justine would sit in the best seats near the umpire's chair with her mother, Francoise, while Jose would take his younger son, Thomas, to sit among the German supporters at the back of the stands. Justine was a 'German supporter' for the day too. Later she explained: 'I already had an enormous admiration for Steffi by then, I even had a poster of her on my wall. I was so sad when she lost to Seles that day.'

But the Henin family had also witnessed what Jose described as 'the match of the century', because Seles had won 6-2, 3-6, 10-8. And there was another reason why Francoise was positively beaming when she met up with her husband again straight afterwards.

'Do you know what Justine said to me?' Francoise whispered to her husband. She looked over to where members of the Graf and Seles families were sitting in the Tribune des Joueurs – the players' seats. 'Then she told me: "One day you'll sit there – you and Papa." And she pointed at the players and said: "I'll be out there."'

By her own admission, Justine actually went a step further than that on the day. She revealed later: 'I remember sitting on centre court and telling her: "I will play here one day and I will win, I will be champion." She probably thought: "This child is dreaming." And I was.'

CHAPTER 19
DEATH AND DESTINY

IN EARLY 1994, FRANCOISE BEGAN TO FEEL UNWELL, AN unusual state of affairs for the strong and charismatic character. Her forceful personality had often made her seem indestructible. Now she was losing weight and finding it hard to digest her food.

The willpower she had shown to keep her unborn baby when Florence was crushed under the car had been truly remarkable. Not even a broken foot could shake her resolve or end her pregnancy. Her elder son, David, owed his life to such determination. So the idea that any physical ailment was getting the better of her seemed foreign somehow. She was so strong, so indomitable, so tough. In fact, her husband sometimes wished she were a little softer with him. But this was Francoise, and above all she was a wonderful mother. The patient side to her nature expressed itself best in her relationship with her children. And she wasn't about to change her priorities for anyone.

Jose explained: 'Sometimes teachers find it hard to leave their professional persona in the classroom and she would be bossy at home too. We had already been through a lot, trying to get over the death of Florence, and at times the strain had almost split us up. But we came through together and we had great moments. We loved each other and we loved our children.'

Knowing that her mother, Bearthe, had died in her early 40s, Francoise might have felt more than the usual apprehension when she went to see the family doctor, Hugues Bastin, about her mystery ailment. Bastin was married to Jose's sister, also called Francoise, and therefore knew this particular patient better as a close relative. One can only imagine his feelings as he sent her to hospital for urgent exploratory tests. Francoise was soon diagnosed with cancer of the colon. It seemed certain that her own children would be forced to endure the same pain that she had as a teenager, losing their mother young, and there was little she could do about it. The illness hadn't been detected in time to do very much for Francoise. This was a sad and familiar story, since cancer can often attack the colon without the victim experiencing any clearly identifiable symptoms in the early stages.

Jose and his wife absorbed the awful reality. After all they had been through, why this? An operation in April 1994 only showed how quickly the disease had spread. The doctors didn't hold out much hope. She might have a year, maybe less. At the end of that time, Justine and the rest of the children would be without a mother.

Francoise and Jose decided to try to keep this awful secret from their children. David, Thomas, Justine and Sarah would be better off not knowing the truth, at least for now, they believed. They would be protected from the finality of their mother's illness until the last possible moment. By doing it their way, Jose and Francoise could give their children time to adapt to the reality that their mother was ill. Francoise herself would also have time to prepare herself for what was to come. For now, they would all carry on as normally as her health would allow. They would enjoy what time was left to them as a family, and try to be like any other. Then, in the final few weeks, they imagined nature would take over.

To carry out such a bold plan required Francoise to show an enormous amount of personal courage. Paying tribute to her in November 2007, Justine said: 'I think a lot about her now and what it must have been like for her. I hate to think about death; I'm scared to die and I can't imagine how tough it must have been for her. But I'm sure she didn't think of that, she just thought about her kids and what was going to become of us.'

In the meantime, however, the immediacy and beauty of every moment with her children would sustain her through the living nightmare, although Justine, her brothers and little sister would only later be able to appreciate the significance of that precious time. But their mother's strength wasn't a façade. Her fighting spirit, her bravery and her consideration for others never wavered. Justine and her siblings would never forget the courage she showed.

Even so, Francoise and Jose couldn't protect their children entirely from what was about to change their lives. Early in this final year of her mother's life, Justine was sufficiently concerned to ask her mother what was wrong with her, but Francoise simply gave her a big hug and said everything would be fine. Perhaps too afraid to probe more deeply, or not wishing to cause her mother further distress, Justine left it at that. But it became increasingly obvious that all was not well.

Mother and child. Justine Henin, in her second year, with her beloved mum, Francoise. They are at the local soccer club in Han-sur-Lesse where, ten years earlier, a victory for the home side had sparked chaotic celebrations, which led to the tragic death of Justine's sister, Florence.

Little Justine is already the centre of attention, and loving every moment. Her father Jose, who is holding her, tended to be overprotective of his second daughter because of what had happened to the first. Justine's brothers complete the line-up here, with Thomas far left and David far right.

Winners. Justine, left, shows off an early trophy alongside her compatriot Olivier Rochus. For Henin there would be many more, while Rochus also made it to the Grand Slam circuit. He attended Justine's wedding to Pierre-Yves Hardenne in 2002, and remains a friend.

Friends and rivals. Justine is 11 years old here, Kim Clijsters ten, though the Flemish girl is already much taller. In time their relationship would be stretched to the limit. But it was Henin who triumphed when they met in Grand Slam finals, due to her ruthlessness.

Emerging talent. Even at the age of nine, Justine was full of flowing shots and steely determination, although it would take her a good few years to develop the physical strength that would help propel her to world number one.

All hail to the new queen of Roland Garros! Justine wins the Junior French Open in 1997, and is clearly enjoying her first taste of true stardom. Winning silverware at this venue became a habit as her career progressed. Ten years after this photo was taken, everyone recognised Justine as the finest clay court player of her generation.

Loving sisters. Justine and Sarah, as close in 1997 as they are now. Justine's feud with her father, Jose, meant that Sarah and Justine spent the best part of seven years hardly seeing each other. Sarah did much of the diplomatic work necessary to achieve her dream of reconciliation.

Thomas and David offer their support to their sporting sister. However, Justine later fell out with both her brothers over Pierre-Yves Hardenne. Only after she separated from her husband in 2007, and David almost died in a car crash, was this trio seen together again.

Good mates. Carlos Rodriguez and Jose Henin got along just fine at first but it was Justine's Argentinian coach who became a father figure. In late 2007 Carlos and Jose buried the hatchet over a beer in Monaco.

Wedding bells, 16 November, 2002. Escorted by Hugues Bastin, husband of her paternal aunt, Francoise, Justine is about to become Henin-Hardenne. Her father, Jose, wanted to lead her down the aisle despite their differences, but the family wasn't invited.

In the zone. Justine is playing with fresh enthusiasm as she launches another fizzing backhand at Roland Garros, 2007. For the first time at a Grand Slam final, her brothers, David and Thomas, and her sister, Sarah, were present to see her win a fourth French Open crown.

Taking America by storm. The delight is there for all to see as Justine lifts the US Open trophy for a second time in 2007. She describes it as her finest Grand Slam victory of all, because on the way to glory she defeated both Williams sisters, Serena and Venus, in their own backyard.

Reunited at last. Justine and Jose Henin step out on to a tennis court together for the first time in seven years. They are in Charleroi, Belgium, in late 2007. Father and daughter grant the author the privilege of securing the first public picture of them since the end of their long, bitter feud.

Justine gratefully accepts the accolade of Sportswoman of the Year, 2007, at the Laureus Sports Awards. Among a star-studded audience in St Petersburg that night were Russia's president, Vladimir Putin, movie legend Dennis Hopper, and England's soccer manager, Fabio Capello.

Jose later said of his children: 'They knew Francoise was ill. We didn't tell the children she had cancer, though, not in so many words. But they knew something serious was happening to their mother. Justine knew like the rest, but she avoided the specifics. She was still young and she didn't ask too many questions.'

Justine threw herself into her tennis, something she knew she could control and understand. At 11, she had already taken Belgium by storm. By 12, she was starting to compete on equal terms with the finest youngsters in Europe, even those with an extra year of competition under their belts. In January 1995, as Francoise felt her strength finally starting to ebb away, Justine began to take her frustration out on her opponents. Jose took her to a big under-14s tournament in Tarbes, in the Pyrenees. It was an indoor competition called the Les Petits As, the top international tournament for 12–14-year-old players. Age didn't seem to matter to a girl desperate to give her mother something to smile about. Sure enough, a delighted Justine was soon able to phone home to tell her mother that she had reached the quarter-finals.

Jose recalled: 'She asked my wife to come down to watch her play her big match. Francoise had to tell Justine that she would find a way to come down if she reached the semi-final. After the call, I phoned back to reassure my sick wife that it was highly unlikely Justine would win her quarter-final. She was just a 12-year-old, up against a Spanish girl (Eva Trujillo) who was older and much bigger.

'Justine went out and won 6-0, 6-0. It was incredible. Nothing was going to stop her. And nothing was going to stop Francoise either. She got in the car and drove 1,200 kilometres to be with her daughter, even though she was only months away from death. She drove all through the night to be there for that semi-final. You have to realise, Francoise was in the advanced stages of a terminal illness. But she wasn't going to let her daughter down, and Justine wasn't going to let her mother down. She caused an even bigger upset to win that semi-final too.'

And typically, she did it in dramatic style. Francoise watched her beat a Hungarian called Zsofia Gubasci 6-4, 2-6, 7-6. She had rewarded Francoise for her nightmare journey. Both had proved their point and demonstrated a bond of almost superhuman strength. Amazing forces of will had been at work.

Reality took over when a big Croatian girl called Mirjana Lucic beat Justine 6-3, 6-2 in the final, though perhaps the emotion of that extraordinary semi-final reunion with her mother had taken its toll on Justine too. As for Francoise, she insisted on making the return journey by car, even though she could have had Jose's air ticket. He, in turn, insisted on driving his exhausted wife so she could get some sleep.

In tennis terms, Tarbes was a fitting farewell, the last time Francoise watched her daughter play. But as far as Justine was concerned, Tarbes was simply the last time others could see her mother watching; she would later behave as though she could feel her mother's presence during some of the biggest matches of her career.

In the weeks after that excursion to the Pyrenees, however, it became clear that time was running out for Francoise. Justine claimed later: 'I was 12, my sister was eight, my brothers were 19 and 21. I wouldn't say it's easier at that age, but they were almost adults. I'm sure that my mum must have worried about that; she would have been scared that the family would . . . well, do what we did, actually. We stopped being a family.' Jose confirmed: 'A few months before her death she told me: "The most important thing is to keep the family united after I'm gone."'

But Francoise harboured another fear, one she shared with Justine before she died. And although their time together was all too short, it stuck in Justine's mind, and you could see her bottom lip quiver slightly, her voice tremble, as she explained. 'I think my mum did a lot for me. I don't have a lot of memories, just a few years of memories with her. But she was pretty scared about the fact that I was giving everything for tennis. She was scared that I would make a lot of sacrifices for nothing.'

That wasn't to suggest for a moment that Francoise didn't believe in her daughter's God-given ability, because she did. But she was also a realist, she knew that injuries or any unforeseen problem could put paid to a young child's dream. While she encouraged Justine to follow her dreams, and to believe in herself, she also wanted her daughter to retain a sense of balance in her life. In the end, poor Francoise knew that it would be down to Justine to work out how a sense of balance survives alongside intense professional ambition, for her own life was nearly over. Francoise decided to see out her last days in Jose's parents' house in the rue de Grottes. Jeanne recalled: 'We told them to come to us and we prepared the bed. I still remember preparing Francoise some eggs two days before she died. The next time I asked her what I could get her, she just said: "Nothing more."'

Jose attempted to prepare his children by leading them out onto the tree-lined track that winds its way towards the Han-sur-Lesse caves. He said: 'I took the children out for a walk and gently told them that their mum was about to leave us and join Florence in Heaven.' Justine took up the story in 2007. 'I'll never forget it,' she recalled. 'He said, "Your mum is going to be reunited with your sister in heaven." I couldn't believe it. I thought he was going to say: "Your mum is going back to the hospital" or "Your mum is going to go somewhere." I knew it, but I didn't want to accept it . . .'

Jeanne and Alphonse watched anxiously from their bedroom window to see how the children would take the news. Almost nine years later, Jeanne remembered the scene all too clearly. She recalled: 'Suddenly we saw the boys take their sisters up in their arms, and we knew then that Jose had broken the news.'

One by one, her children went up to say goodbye, and Francoise told each what a joy they had been in her life. But no one saw Justine go. Alphonse, Jeanne and Jose all tell it the same way. 'I think she was very scared, and that's why she didn't go,' her grandfather suggested. 'And that is quite understandable.' Eventually, Francoise slipped into a coma. Jose movingly recalled: 'I climbed on to the bed then, and lay with her, holding her. She died in my arms the following morning. It was two months before our 25th wedding anniversary.'

Francoise passed away on 26 March 1995. She was 48 years old. Justine didn't react to her mother's death in the way her father had anticipated. He explained: 'After Francoise died, Justine didn't cry – at least I never saw her. At the funeral, instead of tears, she found another way to express her grief. She limped, I believe it was psycho-somatic because I don't believe she was carrying any injury at the time.' Justine admitted: 'Three days after my mum died I was back at school. I wanted to be back in my normal life as soon as possible.'

Jose was still worried for Justine while he was mourning the loss of his wife. 'Her lack of tears, in public at least, caused concern because the family doctor mentioned it to me, a month or two later. He told me that it was important for Justine to cry, to let it all out. But as far as I know, she never did.'

CHAPTER 20
A PROMISE TO KEEP

SOMETHING INSIDE JUSTINE HENIN FROZE THAT DAY, AND it took many years for her to learn to let her emotions show in public. Her immediate impulse was to give up tennis completely. She had carried on playing through her mother's illness, and there had been a sense to it all during those dark days. Tennis had given her a focus away from the unspoken alarm surrounding her mother's deteriorating condition. Her success, she hoped, had given her mother some added determination, and inspiration too. But now she was gone, there seemed no point to it all. Many years later, Justine admitted: 'When my mum died, I thought tennis was over. I wasn't finding any more reason to play.'

Justine was quiet, hiding behind the school routine, withdrawn and devoid of passion. She might have fallen into a more profound depression, but she managed to catch herself just in time, largely by imagining what Francoise would have thought of her subdued behaviour. 'I thought that my mum wouldn't want to see me like this,' she explained simply, and that was the start of the transformation.

The limp that Jose had first noticed at the funeral quickly disappeared, Justine picked up her tennis racket again, and suddenly she was back in touch with life. Perhaps she didn't exhibit the same bubbly nature as she had possessed before the tragedy, but then none of the Henin family was capable of anything approaching joy so soon after what had happened. The main thing for Justine was that she had found a way to function, and even thrive, driven by a newfound strength of character. There was an intensity about her that surpassed even the remarkable focus she had shown when her mother was still alive.

Over the next 18 months the memory of Francoise drove Justine on to greater tennis heights. She realised that she could still play for her mother, even now that she had passed away. Her mission to become one of the sport's greats took on a spiritual dimension, and yet there was an earthly anger about her game to go with her know-how and talent.

Jose, meanwhile, had been hit hard by his wife's death, and continued to mourn her loss, while forcing himself to function for the sake of his children. He did what he could for his daughter's career, and he made sure his other children had what they needed too. Life had to go on, his surviving family was his motivation, and he too found comfort in the pleasure it would have given Francoise to see how Justine continued to progress in the tennis world.

That journey soon led to Carlos Rodriguez in Mons, and Justine's bond with her coach grew stronger with each passing year. Eventually Justine sensed that it was Carlos, not her father, who might make her dream of Roland Garros glory come true. And yet it was her father who was still trying to call so many of the shots in her life. She had to get away, she felt, to give herself the best chance of happiness; in her professional life and in her private life too. Her mother would understand why she was taking such a radical course of action, she felt sure of it. Indeed, when she made the break for independence, Justine's perfectly preserved memories of her mother may have given her further reason to direct her bitterness against her father.

Jose recalled what happened soon after Justine left the family home in 2000. 'Some tactless person chose this moment to tell Justine about some of the problems that had existed in my marriage to her mother. The one-sided way in which the story was told gave Justine a further excuse to do what she wanted. But I repeat, not a day goes by when I don't miss Francoise. And whatever happened in our marriage, I really did love her and she loved me.'

At the time, Justine didn't seem to want to consider the fact that life isn't always as simple as we would like; that perhaps her mother might have been at least partially responsible for any complications in her marriage, since there are two sides to every story. As her uncle Jean-Marie, Jose's brother, put it: 'She looked upon her mother like a saint and still does.' Jose was cast as the villain of the piece, and Justine's anger intensified. Neither was Justine's mother there to question her daughter's abrasive course at this time, or gently persuade her to ask herself whether or not she was doing the right thing by ignoring the rest of the family.

So, feeling alienated, the family were left to watch her career on television. They saw what Justine and the tough Parisian crowd did to Serena Williams in the 2003 French Open semi-final. Jose had mixed feelings about that; but deep down he knew how the death of Justine's mother had hardened her resolve and pushed her game to the edge.

Justine admitted as much later, when she was asked whether she would have been as good a player if her mother hadn't died. She replied with a smile: 'You know, I was talking to my friends about that the other day: what would my life be like now if she hadn't died? Would I be the same player? I don't know. There are things I probably did that I would never have done with her at my side. I'm this woman now because of her and maybe also because she passed away, I will never know. That gave me a lot of character.'

Jose understood why his daughter would have done almost anything to achieve her dream – a final at Roland Garros. Only those who had been at the French Open back in 1992, and then witnessed the final days of Francoise in 1995, could fully understand Justine's motivation. Behind her ice-cold ruthlessness in 2003 was a burning desire to honour her promise to her late mother. Part of the vow had been kept, because she was already in that final; but she had also promised Francoise that she would be champion.

Pierre-Yves hadn't met Justine until 1998, and maybe he didn't know quite what victory in the final of the 2003 French Open, against her old rival Kim Clijsters, would mean to Justine. He lay next to her on the eve of that final in Paris, anticipation heavy in the air and peaceful sleep hard to come by. Justine later revealed that she was woken by noises in the corridor at three in the morning. She tried to get back to sleep, but Pierre-Yves kept coughing. The hours passed. Finally she drifted off again, but she had run out of time. It was morning and soon she was wide awake again, though still feeling tired. In her head, she spoke to her mother. 'You'll have to give me the energy to win today,' she told her.

Then she had a quiet word with herself: 'You'll have to win. You'll have to do it for Mum. Fight all the way. Don't let this escape you.'

She talked it over with her husband. To take the pressure off, he said: 'It's not everything if you win or lose. It doesn't matter. We're very proud of you anyway.'

He must have known deep down that it did matter. It mattered a lot. Even so, his thoughtful remarks still served to remove a little part of the fear of failure that lurks in every finalist's heart. Perhaps Justine's love for her mother would do the rest.

On finals morning, when it is still eerily quiet, each player is allowed practice time on the Court Philippe Chatrier, the centre court. For Justine, these moments were perhaps more special than for any other finalist the tournament will ever know. She revealed later: 'I warmed up for the final that morning and I kept looking over at the spot near the umpire's chair where my mother and I had sat together in 1992. My coach, Carlos Rodriguez, could tell something was happening to me and so I showed him the seats where we watched the match.'

She could almost see herself sitting there with her mother as an awestruck 10-year-old, watching her first major tournament live. What had left the biggest impression on Justine that afternoon had been the sheer determination of Monica Seles and Steffi Graf; their pride, their refusal to bow to the will of the other. Justine had taken much of that on board and underpinned her own game with a similar street-fighting spirit. Taking her mother's courage and willpower into account, that fighting spirit probably wasn't hard to find within herself.

Francoise wouldn't be waiting for her daughter in the

Tribune des Joueurs that afternoon; but Justine was convinced that her mother would be watching from somewhere, giving her the energy to succeed. This final was always meant to be. No one could take it away from her now. With one last look at their 1992 seats, she finished her practice. She was ready.

A few hours later under a cloudless Parisian sky that same arena was packed, and Justine Henin-Hardenne was warming up against the powerful Kim Clijsters, the woman she couldn't seem to beat any more. As for the semi-final, Justine wore a white cap, white top and grey skirt, hoping to let her tennis do the talking. Kim was more eye-catching in a red top, white skirt and white cap. Looking on were King Albert and Queen Paola of Belgium, who had two players to cheer for; Thierry Henry, the world famous footballer; and Australian tennis star Lleyton Hewitt, who was Clijsters' boyfriend at the time. Justine had her husband Pierre-Yves, her aunt Genevieve, her coach Carlos Rodriguez and his little son, Manuel, in her corner. They were all as helpless as each other, those spectators, famous or otherwise. The early blows out on court would be what really counted.

At 30-30 in the first game, Clijsters scored a useful psychological point when she came out of a long and bruising rally the winner. The tense expression on Pierre-Yves' face suggested this wasn't going to be easy. But a fizzing backhand pass from Justine seemed to shake her opponent, and an emphatic smash gave Henin-Hardenne break point. Another fierce return had Clijsters hitting too long: Justine's raw aggression had struck first blood.

Pumped up with adrenalin, Henin-Hardenne began to play wildly on her own service, and suddenly Kim was back in it with three break points. Justine saved one with a beautifully disguised backhand drop-shot, and two unforced errors from Clijsters took care of the rest. A third gave Justine advantage, and Kim screamed 'No!' in horror at what she had done. Henin-Hardenne made a careless mistake of her own, but forgave herself more easily. She made amends with a superb smash and followed up with a decisive ace. It was 2-0 and Kim had blown her big chance. Her head failed to clear in time to save her own service game, and before she knew it she was three games behind.

The sit-down may have given Justine too much time to think about her terrific start, because she imploded straight afterwards. Three inexplicable unforced errors gave Kim as many break points as before. As usual, Henin-Hardenne fought like a tiger when cornered. A colossal serve wiped away the first break point. Two massive forehands bludgeoned Clijsters into further submission, and soon the Flemish girl only had one last chance to break back at 30-40. Justine was playing like a woman possessed, and a stunning series of strokes from the baseline, some executed with both feet off the ground, earned her breathing space at deuce. More power play gave Henin-Hardenne advantage, and a final serve struck the line and stayed low. Game over, 4-0 and Kim was in turmoil, just as she had been in Ostend more than a decade earlier.

Justine's flowing backhand helped her to break point in Clijsters' next service game, and just when Kim needed big serves she produced turkeys. A double-fault to go 5-0 behind must have been beyond her worst nightmares. Pierre-Yves rested his head on his hand and tried not to look too content. Justine swept relentlessly through the next game until she had two set points. The crowd clapped rhythmically, anticipating the first kill of the day. Justine took her second chance with a magical drop-shot, and wrapped up the first set 6-0 in 26 minutes.

It wasn't over. Clijsters had lost a set 6-0 earlier in the tournament and still won. She took the opening game of the second set to sympathetic cheers, but pretty soon Justine had fought back and earned a break point to go 2-1 ahead. She had Kim's drop-shot nailed by now, and dashed in to whip her usual winning reply. Justine was a whirlwind. A smash, an ace and two unforced Clijsters errors consolidated the break at 3-1. But suddenly, staring defeat in the face, the bigger girl began to hit freely, just as she had at Roland Garros two years earlier, when Justine had choked. She struck back to go 3-2, then caused her boyfriend Lleyton Hewitt to climb out of his seat as she battled her way to two break points. Unbelievably, she wasted her chance again, and still seemed to be beating herself up inside when Henin-Hardenne went 4-2 ahead.

Now the scores were exactly as they had been at Roland Garros in that semi-final of 2001 – before the turnaround that had almost resulted in the death of Justine's paternal grandfather, Alphonse. Justine didn't seem to like the home straight, and the next few minutes must have had Jeanne trying to pull her husband, Alphonse, away from their television back in Han-sur-Lesse, before he had another stroke.

With nothing to lose, Clijsters showed all the force and precision that had made her such a great player in the first place. She came back confidently to 3-4, and then asked some serious questions of Justine's nerve. Sure enough, it looked as though the smaller girl was going to choke again. Feeling the pressure and troubled by sudden gusts of wind,

Henin-Hardenne began to misfire on her own serve, massive Clijsters forehands probing her defence. Justine was either hitting too long or too low, she couldn't get it right any more. Doubts crept into her mind, memories of a winning position wasted two years earlier. If she allowed those negative thoughts to snowball, she would soon be facing a dreadful case of déjà vu. When yet another ill-advised Justine shot floated helplessly into the net, Kim was level at 4-4, the momentum firmly with her.

Everyone could sense the makings of a second dramatic comeback in three years, Kim included. She probably imagined her opponent shaking inside, struggling to shut out the fear of choking again in front of the sporting world. But at a time when most players would have crumbled under Clijsters' force, Justine thought of her mother and fought back. She dug in with some desperate returns and refused to be brushed aside. Then, out of nowhere, she produced a vicious cross-court backhand, and clenched her fist when she saw Kim beaten.

Staring across the net at her opponent, the little warrior knew what a telling psychological blow she had just delivered. Sure enough, Kim's mind seemed to go. Two unforced errors later, she had gifted Justine three break points in the most important game of her life. Clijsters saved the first with some belated defiance of her own. But Justine wasn't about to let her off the hook as Kim had done earlier; not when her childhood dream was so close to coming true. This time Justine blasted a forehand winner that brought the house down.

CHAPTER 21
THE MOMENT

JUSTINE WAS ABOUT TO SERVE FOR THE MATCH. SHE could see the finishing line. And then, inexplicably, she served a double-fault. She won the next rally, but Carlos Rodriguez clearly thought she had done so more by luck than merit. When she glanced up, his forefinger jabbed a warning as if to say 'No! That's too tentative!' Then he smacked his fist into his other hand. The message seemed unmistakable. 'Be ruthless! Make it yours!'

A nervous Justine needed a second serve at 15-15, but Clijsters failed to make her pay. It was the Flemish girl's 44th unforced error, and she couldn't expect many more chances. Carlos had demanded one last burst of aggression from Justine. She responded in the next rally with a superb forehand to set up her winning volley. Eleven years down the line, she was almost there. Justine had two match points with which to fulfil the vow she had made to her mother.

Clijsters returned the next serve with power, but the ball struck the ribbon of the net and rebounded into the air. It might have landed just over the net, which would have left

Justine little or no time to come in. Instead, as if nudged by a force from above, the ball came down on Kim's side. It was over, a lifetime's ambition realised in 67 minutes, the moment almost too big to take in.

There was a split second of silence before Justine and the rest of Roland Garros realised she was champion. Then she threw away her racket, turned her back on Clijsters and cradled her head in her arms. As she looked up, in those first moments, there can be little doubt that she was thinking of her mother. In the Tribune des Joueurs, where Jose's wife would have been sitting had she still been alive, Pierre-Yves tried to hug Carlos. But the coach hardly responded, he was too busy punching the air in triumph. So Justine's husband did the same, shaking one fist and then both at the same time, wild lunges in the direction of the court. Pierre-Yves finally got to hug Carlos at about the same time as Clijsters sportingly hugged Justine at the net.

Kim knew her opponent's history and she realised what this meant to her. Clijsters had wanted victory badly, but deep down she might not have wanted it quite as much as Justine. Perhaps only tragedy can give you that kind of hunger. Could Justine feel her mother's presence? She thought so. Now she looked close to tears, and glanced up at Pierre-Yves and Carlos. Not wanting to wait a moment longer to be with them, she disappeared down the tunnel, to the slight confusion of the crowd. When she suddenly emerged near the seat she had once promised to her mother, everyone understood. Pierre-Yves had gone, but he reappeared just in time. She hugged him as hard as she could, and she hugged Carlos too. Soon all three embraced as one, to rapturous applause from the Roland Garros crowd. This trio had been a team. Now they were a winning team, and no one would ever be able to take this victory away from them.

Justine broke free briefly to embrace her aunt Genevieve before falling back into the arms of an ecstatic Pierre-Yves. Though he didn't seem to want to let go, she knew she had to return to the court below to receive her trophy. Her defeated opponent no doubt wanted to get the formalities out of the way.

There was a big cheer for Clijsters as she received the runner-up plate and two kisses from Prince Albert of Belgium, who was dressed in a khaki suit. But an even bigger cheer greeted his kisses for Justine; and as she raised the Suzanne Lenglen trophy high above her head she must have worn the widest grin in Paris.

There was a sense of expectation when Justine took hold of the microphone to speak to the crowd. 'Thank you,' she said, pausing for more cheers. 'I'm very honoured to be here with you at Roland Garros, a place which evokes such powerful emotions inside me. Thank you for your support. The first Grand Slam is for you all.' Having complimented Kim on her performance and thanked the officials and sponsors, Justine came to those matters closest to her heart. 'I'd like to give my personal thanks to two people now. They are true companions when the going gets tough, Pierre-Yves, my husband, and Carlos, my coach.'

As the crowd applauded, Pierre-Yves smiled through his tears and then had to look down, clearly overcome. But this was just the beginning. Both he and Carlos, who had his son, Manuel, sitting on his shoulders by now, must have known what was coming.

'I want the last words I say to you to be about my mother, to whom I dedicate this win. My mum is looking down at me from Paradise. I hope you are very proud of me, Mum!' As she spoke these words, Justine put her hand on her heart and her eyes filled, though she managed to maintain her self-control. Up in the box, Pierre-Yves promptly burst into tears and covered his face. Justine kissed the Suzanne Lenglen trophy like a long-lost friend and posed for hordes of photographers. The dream had come true. Most of her life had been lived for these unforgettable seconds. When someone with an image as hard as Justine's reveals such emotion, it somehow carries extra power.

The woman, the warrior, the chief breadwinner, held aloft her prize while her partner, the man of the family, simply melted in tears. A more complete reversal of roles you could scarcely expect to see, even in the tough world of sport. Yet there was no disgrace in Pierre-Yves' tears; they enhanced the moment and showed how much he loved his wife. However Hardenne behaved before or after this moment, and whatever happened subsequently in the relationship between Pierre-Yves and Justine, this is the enduring image of the love they shared for a good many years.

As for Jose, listening to the victory speech back home, this was a strange moment. He said later: 'It was right that she spoke about her mother and the others, I have no argument with that. But I was hoping she would find a way to thank me, too, perhaps even without mentioning me by name. She could just have said that she wanted to thank other people who could not be there for whatever reason, people who had helped her in the past. And I would have understood that she also meant me. But there was nothing at all.'

Justine knocked back one journalist who wanted her to offer her father an olive branch. She did so with all the force of one of her fastest backhands. 'I took decisions a long time ago and they were the right decisions. I have the people I want around me. That's the most important thing, you know. In life you have to make choices, even if they're hard. You don't live in the past . . .'

But that last remark was a little ironic, given that her victory had been inspired by the past like no other. It had been her destiny, her biggest target for 11 long years. Justine took what she wanted, what she needed from her past in order to succeed that day at Roland Garros. And what she needed at the time was not her father, or indeed the rest of her living family, with the complications they brought to the table; what she needed was the simple, loving memory of her mother.

Would she have taken that title had her mother not died? In 2007 she didn't sound convinced. 'I'd be a good tennis player,' she acknowledged, 'but would I be that champion with that personality? No, I'm not quite sure. I never wanted to take revenge on life. Life is beautiful; life has brought me good things and I would love to be able to share them with my mum, but she is gone and she will never be back, but she lives inside me and I want to live my life the best I can, so she can be proud.'

On that glorious day at Roland Garros, Justine was proud too. She was proud that she had been able to justify all the sacrifices she had made; proud that she had in her arms that precious trophy, something tangible at the end of all her suffering, the Grand Slam title she had always dreamed of. Above all, Justine was proud to have shown that her obsessive dedication to tennis as a child hadn't all been for nothing, as her mother had understandably feared it might have been.

CHAPTER 22
MATCH OF THE CENTURY

THEY SAY WHAT GOES AROUND COMES AROUND. WHEN Justine Henin-Hardenne first saw Jennifer Capriati dressed in all-American red skirt and blue top with white stars, she must have known the crowd would be as partisan as the baying Paris mob who had helped her through her last Grand Slam semi-final. But this was the semi-final of the 2003 US Open, not the French, and the Flushing Meadows fans would be cheering for the woman on the other side of the net. Justine had chosen white, but under the bright floodlights that evening she definitely wasn't cast as the heroine of the piece.

Capriati's story was almost as remarkable as Justine's. She had first reached the US Open semi-final some 12 years earlier, the year before Justine went to Roland Garros as a child with her mother. Twice she had served for the match against Monica Seles, before losing the final set in a tie-break. Jennifer had then descended into substance abuse, only to pull herself back up for another semi-final appearance a decade later against Venus Williams. Once again she was denied at the death, and 2003 very possibly represented her last real chance to take the title.

Matthew Perry, star of the hit television sit-com *Friends*, was in Capriati's corner along with her father Stefano, a big, flat-nosed bruiser of a man who looked like he had a temper. Apart from them, Justine had to contend with thousands of boisterous American fans that wanted to see her crash and burn. The trick was to try and silence them from the start, and when Justine exploded into a 4-1 lead she appeared to have done just that.

But Capriati struck back, an awesome forehand pass and a deadly smash helping her to break point in the very next game. Justine's first serve was a fault, and an American fan applauded. As Justine feared, the events of Paris and the taunting of Serena Williams had not been forgotten this side of the Atlantic. Unsettled, Justine missed a great chance to get out of trouble, hitting inexplicably long. Capriati was back in the set at 2-4.

Dramatic rallies and superb volleys filled the next game, and the power of Capriati's forehand helped the American to reduce the deficit to 3-4. Controversy arrived in the eighth, when British umpire Alison Lang overruled a baseline judge to call Henin-Hardenne's shot out, even though a computerised replay showed it had hit the back of the line. A wild backhand saw the beleaguered Justine broken for the second time in succession, and now they were even at 4-4.

Capriati fought back from 0-30 down to win her fourth game in a row, meaning Justine had to serve to stay in the first set. A 12-stroke epic soon confirmed the breathtaking quality of the match, which was already developing into a classic. Gripped by hysteria, the crowd screamed 'Out!' mid-rally as Henin-Hardenne's brave pass flirted with the line. Another of her shots flicked the net, allowing Capriati to take control of the point. Justine resorted to a desperate backhand on the half-volley, but Jennifer raced up to kill the point to huge cheers.

Facing two set points, Justine's first serve was a fault and this time more of the crowd dared to applaud her mistake. Capriati latched onto the second serve to force more pressure and Henin-Hardenne hit long when it mattered. The stadium erupted; the all-American girl had claimed five games in a row to take the first set 6-4. Her father was on his feet and Jennifer allowed herself a smile during the changeover.

Justine stared her granite stare, bit her lip and planned her comeback, breaking serve immediately when play resumed. But Capriati was soon over the shock and came up with more scintillating tennis during that second set to go 4-3 ahead. Two unforced errors and a Capriati forehand left Justine facing three break points, and she could only save one. Jennifer would serve for the match at 5-3, and she openly jumped for joy at the thought. With her fans roaring her on, it seemed as though the job was done already. Although nerves inevitably crept into that all-important game, at 30-30 Capriati knew that she was two points from glory.

Daringly, Justine came up with a drop-shot at full stretch on the half-volley, and earned herself a precious break point. Capriati came up with a fantastic lob which looked unanswerable, but a scampering Henin-Hardenne responded with a seemingly impossible backhand lob of her own. It so shocked Jennifer that she snatched at her next shot and sent it wide. Justine was back at 5-4, and raced on to close her service game with a stretching backhand volley. 'Allez!' she screamed, raising both hands in the air. Jennifer looked sick.

From 5-5 the mesmerising war of attrition continued, the crowd scarcely able to take in the quality of the theatre to which they were being treated. A straight-sliced backhand drop-shot gave Justine the advantage, and she broke with a return that was lethal in its depth. Capriati was broken again and seemed to remonstrate with her family between games. What could she do against this sort of iron will? For the moment the answer was not much. Justine swept through her service game to take the second set 7-5. After 108 minutes of pure drama, during which both women had thrilled Flushing Meadows and millions watching on television, they were all square, drenched in sweat and exhausted.

Justine unleashed a dazzling cross-court backhand to break immediately in the final set, and with so little support in the stadium she raised her arms and cheered herself. But Capriati hit back to earn her own break point, and played her part in a titanic tear-up with no fewer than 14 strokes whipped into every corner of the court. At the end of it, a revitalised Jennifer executed a cold smash to bring the scores level again. An ace gave Jennifer the lead at 2-1, and another baseline blitz saw Justine fire wide to hand her opponent break point. Her mind apparently in turmoil, the little Belgian served into the net. 'Yeah, one more,' yelled an American, willing the double-fault. Henin-Hardenne didn't oblige, hauling herself back to deuce. But Jennifer wouldn't give in and conjured a magical forehand pass on the run. Now she was jumping about like a kangaroo and completed the break to go 3-1.

The home supporters were going crazy when Capriati held serve for 4-1, and once again a match full of aggression and adventure looked over. Justine found a temporary foothold but Jennifer's awesome forehand sent her 5-2 ahead. She was still so pumped up that when she reached the chair she battered the towel as well. More ominously, she wasn't smiling any more.

Hobbling with cramp, Henin-Hardenne allowed Capriati to come back to deuce, leaving the American two points from victory yet again. By the time that game was over there had been five tantalising deuces, as Justine hovered on the edge of oblivion and finally brought herself back to 3-5 with two big serves. Capriati was still serving for the match and the crowd roared her on, but she blew up on the vital game, firing almost everything too low. Now it was 4-5 and Henin-Hardenne was back in the hunt. Incredibly, however, a double-fault left Justine two points from defeat again. Just when Capriati appeared to have earned a match point from the next epic rally with what looked for all the world like a crushing winner, Justine pulled out a seemingly supernatural return to deny her. On they went for 19 stunning strokes, until Justine came up with the decisive forehand.

Henin-Hardenne closed out for 5-5, Jennifer aced for 6-5, and both women were nearly out on their feet by the time they reached their chairs. But Jennifer didn't dare sit down in case she was struck by the cramp now seizing her opponent. Entertainment? These moments were gifts from the sporting gods, and no one wanted to catch the last train back to New York City. Henin-Hardenne was two points from defeat again at 15-30 when they resumed, and pulling up in agony after just about every point. But when Capriati should have gone for the jugular, she allowed her rival to cling on for the tie-break at 6-6.

There was something inside Jennifer that prevented her from taking the tennis rewards she deserved when it really mattered. With Justine vulnerable to the killer blow, Jennifer came up with a full array of shots – all unforced errors. She virtually gifted Henin-Hardenne a winning position at 6-2 with four match points. The disbelieving expression on her father's face may have held the key. You couldn't blame the fearsome-looking Stefano Capriati for the way he looked that night; but Justine, by contrast, only had herself to please, feeling no pressure from Pierre-Yves.

Not that Henin-Hardenne had completely conquered her nerves, as she blew out a breath and looked at the dark New York sky. Was she praying? Justine whipped a backhand into the net and felt new pain in her leg. She hobbled, limped and took another serve. Capriati fought for her life and Justine's next backhand flew wide. Two match points thrown away, two left. Justine looked up at Carlos and Pierre-Yves. The coach clapped his hands together and gave her a reassuring nod. As usual Pierre-Yves followed suit.

In one final clash of wills, Henin-Hardenne sent Capriati the wrong way with a forehand down the line. Jennifer stretched to adjust her shape, and sent a lunging backhand towards the top of the net. The ribbon sent the ball back in her direction. It was over. Justine threw her racket away, fell to her knees and held her head in her hands. Alison Lang read out the score, 4-6, 7-5, 7-6. The spectators howled their appreciation for one of the greatest matches of all time.

Minutes later, Justine was on a drip. On the verge of collapse, she was rushed to the US Open's medical centre, the drip still attached to her arm. The final against Kim Clijsters was due to start in 20 hours. She was in danger of missing it completely. 'I'll go on court if I'm able to compete,' she vowed. 'I'm so tired but I'm very, very happy. And I know my mother is fully aware of what I'm doing.'

CHAPTER 23
GETTING EVEN

THAT STARE. JUSTINE WAS LIKE A BOXER PSYCHING OUT an opponent before a world title bout. She had already gone to work on Kim and they hadn't even decided who would serve first. So much for being too exhausted and dehydrated to make the final. The fatigue was still there, but Justine was running on adrenalin and anger.

Clijsters was now world number one, even though she had never won a Grand Slam. She had broken Serena Williams' 57-week reign with sheer consistency. But it wasn't jealousy that was causing the Henin-Hardenne stare. It was Kim's suggestion that Justine had feigned injury in their recent meeting in San Diego, when she had called the WTA tour trainer to treat blisters on her right foot, having lost the first set 6-3, and then gone on to win the match 3-6, 6-2, 6-3.

After that match Kim had been asked about the unscheduled time-out, and had said: 'I'm sort of getting used to it. She's probably (called for a trainer) in every match that I've played against her. It's just a matter of knowing if it's really for an injury or if she's doing it (for another reason). It didn't look like it was hurting.'

Well Justine had certainly been hurting against Capriati. But following those stinging insinuations from Clijsters, she had tried to make a point of playing through the pain barrier without taking treatment, and it had almost cost her. In those short hours between semi-final and final, Justine had told reporters about her dilemma during the struggle against Jennifer. Henin-Hardenne had said: 'A lot of people have talked badly about me in the last few weeks. So I made a big mistake. I needed a trainer and I will not make a mistake like that again.'

There were no prizes for guessing whom Justine blamed for her own distress. It was in the stare. With a ready smile, she had waltzed up to the stern-looking umpire, Lynn Welch, and even asked how she was. But when Clijsters joined them, her mood suddenly changed and the charm disappeared. Justine's smile froze, faded, and she stared Kim out. Suddenly Clijsters was looking nervous and awkward.

Seconds later, Kim and her rival were told to stand shoulder to shoulder and pose for pictures. Clijsters tried to make a little joke at her own expense, openly wondering which way to turn for the final round of snapshots. Justine smiled efficiently for the cameras and completely ignored her opponent's casual remark. Kim twisted her upper body away, perhaps out of embarrassment, and shot Henin-Hardenne just a hint of a wounded glance before retreating to her side of the net. The psychological battle had been so one-sided so far that it was difficult to imagine the final going any other way, especially when Justine took a 4-2 lead in the opening set. However, Kim fought back to 4-3, then set up break points with an awesome backhand lob from the baseline and a bullet of a forehand pass. In the rally that followed, Justine aimed too low with a swipe and Kim had broken to level the scores at 4-4.

With Clijsters in full flow, Pierre-Yves chewed hard and looked more physically shattered than his wife. Carlos Rodriguez rubbed his eyes and seemed fed up as the match began to drift away from his player. Kim produced strong serves and violent volleys, defiant defence and punishing passes as she claimed her third game in a row to move 5-4 ahead. 'Come on!' she screamed, and clenched her fist in excitement at what she had begun to achieve at last.

Serving to stay in the set, Justine double-faulted to fall 0-30 behind; she miscued a forehand at 15-30 to gift her compatriot two set points. After her heroics against Capriati a few hours earlier, there seemed to be nothing left in the tank. If Henin-Hardenne were to lose this set, it hardly seemed to matter if she won the second; for there would be little hope of her summoning sufficient energy to give a decent account of herself in a third and final set so soon after the epic with Jennifer. Justine understood, and dug deep to serve a sizzling ace straight down the middle. But Clijsters found an ominous rhythm during the rally that developed on the remaining set point. Justine resorted to desperate defence on the baseline, stretching for last-ditch returns under heavy fire. And then, for no apparent reason, Kim snatched at a backhand and sent the ball flying a full metre too long. Justine gave her plenty of time to think about those two wasted set points before she served again.

Now the famous Henin-Hardenne backhand came into play. Her first landed deep in a corner and the second was a spectacular winner. Kim sent her next return sailing from the court, and her chance had gone. Against the odds, a seemingly drained Justine had saved the day at 5-5. That fragile Clijsters confidence had been shattered again, and in the next game she fired too long three times in a row to gift Justine as many break points. A deadly backhand volley confirmed the vital break at 6-5.

When a Clijsters return drifted long on Justine's serve, the French-speaking side of Belgium celebrated wildly. Henin-Hardenne had two set points. 'Allez!' yelled Justine, and Kim botched her next approach shot to throw the set away. Justine jumped for joy and clenched her fist, hardly believing the 7-5 scoreline herself. She had escaped from oblivion, she was a set ahead, and if she could repeat the feat – preferably without quite so much drama – she would be US champion. Justine dashed off for a toilet break, escorted by officials, leaving Kim ample time to wonder where it had all gone wrong.

Clijsters' capacity for shooting herself in the foot was on show again in the very first game of the second set, as she allowed herself to be broken from 40-15. Justine piled on the misery by holding serve to go 2-0 ahead, then found a breathtaking backhand lob under pressure for 3-0. More confident winners made it 4-0, by which time Henin-Hardenne had taken seven games in a row. Justine looked up at the sky, as if in thanks.

Kim showed some belated fighting spirit to change the pattern, take a game and bludgeon her way to a break point for 4-2. Justine seemed to sense that she might not have sufficient reserves of energy to cope with a sustained come-back. Lip-readers reckoned she mouthed two words to herself before she took her next serve – 'Pour Maman' – 'For Mum'. Whatever source of energy she drew upon, it worked. The serve was good enough to entice Kim into over-hitting her return, and Justine went on to win the game. It was 5-1, and Henin-Hardenne was on the verge of achieving Mission Impossible.

She was also on the point of changing her husband's motorbike-riding habits for the duration of their marriage. Pierre-Yves loved to ride his Honda 900 on public roads as well as private tracks. It acted as a thrilling release from the pressurised world of the tennis circuit, and a life dominated by his wife's career. On the bike he was master of his own destiny, and he didn't seem too worried by the widely known statistics that pointed to a shorter life expectancy for petrol heads on two wheels. But Justine was worried. She had known enough death already, and didn't want to lose the man around whom she had built her life off the court.

'She detested the idea of me riding that motorbike on the roads,' Pierre-Yves told me in 2004. But then she had come up with an idea that would give her added motivation for her latest Grand Slam challenge.

'What if I win the US Open?' she had asked. 'Will you reconsider if I take the title in New York?'

Pierre-Yves decided to play along. 'She got me to promise that I would no longer ride my motorbike on public roads if she won the US Open.'

So now Justine was just one game away from getting her way, and taking control of Pierre-Yves' keys to his beloved Honda.

Clijsters already seemed beaten in her own head, and indiscipline on her serve gifted Justine two championship points. Henin-Hardenne looked up at the sky, as if in new prayer, and gazed across at Kim. With the noise of the crowd ringing in her ears, Justine watched as Kim prepared to serve, then raised her hand. Kim didn't seem to see her, so Justine did it again. Clijsters tried to ignore the hand signal and played on. Predictably, her first serve was a fault. The second serve sparked a mighty rally, with Justine firing deadly shots into both corners. She finished it with a magnificent volley on the run, and threw both hands in the air. She laughed as Pierre-Yves hugged Carlos, and then blew her husband a kiss.

Finally, Justine used mime to re-create the action of turning a key in the ignition of a motorbike. And she gestured for Pierre-Yves to hand over her prize.

CHAPTER 24
THE DANGEROUS PEAKS

THE NIGHT JUSTINE WON THE US OPEN, HER FATHER Jose and sister Sarah watched with a mixture of pride and frustration in their modest apartment, tucked away down a side street in the Belgian town of Marche-en-Famenne. They were pleased for her, and yet they knew there would be no trans-Atlantic phone call to include them in the celebrations. Jose suspected that, in his own case at least, there would be no more contact – ever.

Sarah so wanted her sister back, and she would never give up hope of them all being a family again. She wanted that for her father too, knowing how much it hurt him to be left on the outside of Justine's life. But the more famous the tennis star became, the more obvious it was to others that she remained steadfastly opposed to any contact with Jose, and that was the central problem. Life had been good to Justine Henin-Hardenne since she left home.

Jose was both delighted and tormented by his daughter's victories, knowing what he would have to deal with the day after Grand Slam glory. He explained: 'You know what I just can't stand any more? People who come up to me in the street and congratulate me. "Congratulations on Justine's victory! It's wonderful. Allez JuJu. Congratulations!" I can't bear it. They know we don't talk any more, but they still feel they have to come up and say it. I don't feel part of this any more, but I still can't help watching her big matches on television.'

Justine's brother Thomas was also plagued by conflicting emotions at this time. Waves of bitterness engulfed him, to such an extent that sometimes he felt like disowning the tennis star completely. Then, when the hurt subsided for a while, he admitted: 'I miss Justine. But it's the old Justine I miss, not the new one. The new one is a stranger.'

Although she was apparently oblivious to the suffering of her closest relatives, Justine would have agreed with the last part of that remark. After her US Open win, she said: 'I am a different person and a different player since my marriage. I'm just feeling so confident, you know, with my husband. It was very important for me to get married. A lot of things changed in my life. So he's with me almost all the time. I think it's easier . . . It's great to have a family. It gives me a lot of confidence. I'm feeling more secure. I know that after tennis, I'll have something that's very important.'

And what a career she would have to look back on, that much was already clear. Victory over Capriati had ensured that Henin-Hardenne would finish the year as number one in the world, only the 13th undisputed queen of tennis in WTA history. At the tender age of 21, she was honoured alongside some of the all-time-greats of the women's game in a ceremony at the Staples Center in Los Angeles. She high-fived with Martina Navratilova and rubbed shoulders with Chris Evert. She was also congratulated by the legendary Billie Jean King, one of her greatest admirers.

How Francoise would have loved to see her daughter standing there in the spotlight alongside the goddesses of the game. And one word summed up the expression on her face better than any other: satisfaction. This, you sensed, was the moment when her sporting achievements during an amazing year started to sink in. Deep down, however, she must also have known that her mother would have been sad to see the Henin family still locked in conflict. And while Justine clearly believed that Francoise would have understood her need for space, others weren't convinced.

'I'm not so sure her mother would be proud of everything she has done,' said her uncle Jean-Marie without malice. 'When she died, Francoise was forced to leave behind her children, and I don't see how she would be proud that Justine has ignored several members of her family by choice.'

It was a powerful point, and one the Henin family hoped Justine might be prepared to consider in time. They waited patiently, knowing they would all happily embrace her if she ever felt ready to acknowledge them again. Even in January 2004, her surviving grandparents, Alphonse and Jeanne, said: 'Our door is always open to her. The family home should never be closed to a child.' Her uncle, Jean-Paul, echoed: 'If she came into my restaurant now, I would make her perfectly welcome.'

Meanwhile Justine headed for the other side of the world and the Australian Open. She was obviously thinking deeply about others, even if her immediate family didn't fall into that altruistic sphere. At a warm-up tournament in

Sydney, she gave a press conference and highlighted her efforts to improve the lot of some young people who were very close to her heart because of what they were going through. She explained: 'I have a foundation. In French it's "Les Vingt Coeurs de Justine". I'm going to meet some kids who have cancer. So it's a great opportunity for me, because I want to give them a little bit of time.' In English Justine's foundation became known as 'Justine's Winners' Circle', and the goal was to give financial assistance to families with sick children, to make the dreams of those young people come true where possible, and to arrange meetings between the children and her.

Justine's cancer charity wasn't some cynical PR stunt; she clearly had a very caring side to her character, and was more than ready to give her love to people who were suffering like her own mother had. This was Justine's way of reacting positively to the worst emotional trauma of her life, and it was to her eternal credit that she was actively doing something to make the lives of those unfortunate children a little bit better.

So Justine continued to live her life separately, show compassion in her own way, and develop as a person free from family obligations. She knew all about the personal devastation that cancer can cause and would later talk about how much she missed her family at this time. However, she was still not ready for a reunion. Just what she was missing became clear to me in mid-January 2004, when I was invited to attend Sarah's 17th birthday dinner, a family celebration held in the apartment she shared with her father in Marche.

Jose cooked a superb chicken dinner for his daughter, and Justine's name was very much off the menu for the entire evening. Thomas and David were there with their partners, and every member of the Henin family was in sparkling form. That apartment positively glowed with love, warmth and the joy of life, and I couldn't help but think that, for all the success she was achieving on the tennis circuit, Justine was in fact the loser in all this.

The climb to the top of her sporting mountain had been intense, but now she was there. Her tennis gurus would tell her that staying on the peak would be even harder than getting there. In that sense the challenge was only just beginning. But how many trophies would she have to acquire before she realised that they all meant nothing in comparison to the love of a family? At what point would she realise that she was taking a very grave risk by choosing the life she had, where sporting excellence and the respect that went with it seemed to drive everything and exclude so many? Alphonse and Jeanne were getting on in years, and there was no guarantee that the open door which awaited Justine in their warm home would remain that way forever. How awful it would be if her grandparents were no longer around to welcome and reassure her when she was ready to return.

Despite everything, those who sat around the table for Sarah's 17th birthday party remained loyal to the missing Justine. When the party was over, David, the brother who would lie at death's door three years later, admitted that he was preparing to disrupt his sleep pattern to follow Justine's latest attempt to achieve Grand Slam glory, this time in Melbourne. Always the gentleman, David confided: 'We who have not been afforded the slightest contact for the last couple of years will continue to get up in the middle of the night to support her.'

If only there had been a way of impressing upon Justine just how much there was for her to appreciate back home. But she didn't like to talk about her family at all in those days, certainly not with a journalist. She was young and headstrong, you could see the stage she was at in life, and you could understand her confidence, an aura that had grown so strong that she appeared to be bordering on invincibility. Besides, she was going to be rather busy for a few weeks. There was another Grand Slam beckoning.

CHAPTER 25
SEEING IT OUT

'OUT!' SHE CRIED, WAVING HER FINGER AT THE UMPIRE'S chair. 'Out!' Her eyes were insistent now. 'Out! It's out!' There was no let-up in the verbal volley, no room for contradiction. It was the final of the 2004 Australian Open in the Rod Laver Arena, Melbourne Park. Four times in three seconds, Justine Henin-Hardenne had bombarded umpire Sandra de Jenken with a claim that subsequently seemed breathtaking in its audacity, given the subsequent evidence beamed around the world by television, which strongly suggested the ball had struck the baseline.

Doubtless Justine was so anxious to win her third Grand Slam title that she genuinely thought she had seen a drive volley from Kim Clijsters land long. With all the authority of a world number one, she wagged her finger in protest and made the call for the umpire. The stakes were obviously high, and the umpire saw it the same way as Justine, overruling her baseline judge who had remained silent all along. Instead of deuce, it was game over. For Clijsters, the television evidence came too late and she was unable to sustain a second remarkable comeback.

Justine had taken the first set 6-3, and led 4-2 and 15-0 in the second. At that point Clijsters had begun to land blows from all angles, and stormed through to even the match with a 6-4 set against all the odds. Justine had been cruising again in the third, 4-0 and 30-15 ahead, just six snappy shots from glory. But she had imploded again as Kim, backed by an enthusiastic Australian crowd, set about turning the match on its head a second time. Clijsters had broken back twice to claw her way to 3-4, and now she only needed to hold her serve to achieve parity.

Her opponent knew just how dangerous the situation was. She had won from 0-4 down in the first set of her quarter-final against Lindsay Davenport. She risked falling victim to a similar turnaround. Henin-Hardenne's tennis skills had earned her a break point, now her mind games had done the rest. By rights Kim should still have been in there, two strong serves from 4-4 in that final set. Instead she trailed 3-5 and it looked as though all her hard work had been for nothing.

Justine's father knew there would be an inquest later in the media. 'Not good, and not for the first time,' he said, remembering the infamous raised hand against Serena the previous year at Roland Garros. However, he also acknowledged that Justine was within her rights to query the call, and that the umpire had supported her.

True to his word, Justine's eldest brother David was also watching in the middle of the night back in Belgium. 'Is this fair play?' he asked himself. Maybe not, but Justine didn't make the final decisions. This was the cut-throat world of big-time tennis and you had to scrap for everything you got. If you didn't scrap, you didn't get. 'Did you see that out?' was all Kim asked the umpire. De Jenken assured her that she had.

As the Melbourne Park crowd booed loudly, Clijsters shook her head and accepted the apparent injustice of it all. Given that 15,000 fans were ready to back her, she didn't argue her case with sufficient vehemence. Preferring to maintain a sporting dignity, Kim simply got on with the match, and Justine closed out 6-3, 4-6, 6-3.

In a signature routine, the winner threw away her racket and dropped to her knees, burying her face into the green court as if she were about to cry. She didn't, though you could understand the relief behind her gesture. Up in the VIP seats Pierre-Yves clenched his fists, clearly still getting a thrill out of his wife's success.

Kim, who always was just a little too nice for the professional circuit – something she can be proud of for the rest of her life – offered her arch-rival two kisses and reflected upon yet another final defeat. Meanwhile Justine sat down to savour the moment, her face in her hands.

Back in Belgium, Jose's love for his daughter burned away at the big freeze that still kept them apart. 'Justine is the best. I got up at 3.00am Belgian time to watch it on my own. My other children were away in various places, but I think they all watched it too. We promised not to watch Justine again, but it is impossible. She got so far ahead she stopped playing, and that is typical Justine. She has been doing it ever since she was small.'

At her post-match press conference, Clijsters was asked whether she felt that Henin-Hardenne's 'out' calls might have influenced the umpire to overrule on the vital point. 'I'm not going to go into things like that,' she said. 'I don't want to start any trouble. Things happen.' Kind-hearted Clijsters wasn't about to criticise Sandra de Jenken either. She added: 'I'm not going to blame the umpire, because everybody makes mistakes, but of course it is disappointing. A few people have seen the shot on television and told me it was in. So that is even more disappointing.'

Justine was busy showing off the Daphne Akhurst trophy, named after the five-times Australian champion from the 1920s, to the posse of photographers. But it was too heavy to keep above her head for long, and besides it was time for her to face the written media too.

Asked how crucial the umpire's overrule had been to her victory, she gave this unguarded answer: 'Well, it was important because it was a break. And I needed a game after losing three in a row. The umpire took her responsibilities, and I think it was a very tough call, but I think it was just long. It's very hard to say, you know . . .' The journalist tried to press her, but Justine held her ground. 'I was pretty sure, yes. That's why I said it was long, from my point of view. The umpire was pretty sure too. I haven't looked at the film and right now I don't care too much about this.'

As holder of three of the four Grand Slam titles in January 2004, there was no reason why she should care. The record books wouldn't speak of close calls or controversy, and neither would her bank account. Justine's career earnings had now risen to $6,957,559 – not bad for a young woman still in her 22nd year at the time. But for Henin-Hardenne tennis had never been about money. It was about honouring her mother's memory and doing the very best she could. It was about proving she could be number one in the world.

She had done that, just as she had told her mother Francoise she would. The predictions of the little girl who spent hours hitting a tennis ball against the kitchen wall and entire days playing at her local tennis club had come true. Francoise had always smiled and told Justine she was right, she would be the best. Now the target was to stay on top, and it seemed that nothing could stand in her way. She had every shot in the book, the mentality of a street-fighter, and she had developed a physical strength that was staggering for a woman of her size. All she had to do was stay healthy, and she could soon turn into one of the true greats of the game.

As Justine knew only too well, however, good health was not something you could guarantee, no matter how hard you worked on your fitness. She was about to learn that, and her reign as queen of the courts was soon to be threatened like never before.

CHAPTER 26
THE HARDEST GOLD

IT WASN'T EVEN SPRING AND THE WHISPERS WERE THAT Justine's career was over. The word coming from some of those still close to her wasn't much more encouraging. Even though they hoped she might be able to make some sort of return to the professional game in the future, there were no guarantees.

She was seriously ill, that was the general feeling. Whatever had laid her low had sapped almost all the strength and spirit out of her, so that she was almost unrecognisable as the sporting force that had taken the tennis world by storm. In the previous year she had made almost all her tennis dreams come true. Now all she wanted to do was sleep.

Some were more pessimistic than others; but it was difficult for anyone to be optimistic when Justine was finding it a struggle to get up, walk to the bathroom and lift a toothbrush for long enough to clean her teeth. There were times when the idea of lifting a tennis racket again must have seemed a million miles away. The girl whose nimble, dancing feet had moved across a court with more agility than the game had ever seen could barely move at all. Some days she feared she would never play a serious match again. More often she had to confront the nagging suspicion that her predicament might be even more cruel than that, and threaten long-term torture for a tennis perfectionist. For the most likely scenario appeared to be this: she might regain enough fitness over time to return to the circuit, and then find she had lost that extra something, the physical and psychological edge which had previously driven her to the top. For a Grand Slam champion who knew what it was like to be number one in the world, the prospect of tennis mediocrity was probably more horrific than outright retirement.

She retreated into a shell, and even her customary strength of character and determination seemed to desert her. As her body shut down, so in some ways did her personality. She was used to putting so much energy into her friendships, now she felt as though she had precious little to give. Justine herself said of that black period: 'I thought it was the end of my tennis and I worried that I'd never be the same player again. I didn't know what my future was going to be. Even as a person I could feel myself changing. I just wanted to stay at home and not see anyone, not even my friends.'

The nightmare was hard to accept when it was only a matter of weeks since her Australian Open triumph. But the rigorous demands of her climb to the top of women's tennis over the previous year, all the training and playing, week after week, month after month, appeared to have taken their toll. When all the medical tests had been done, and the results came back, there was at least a name to put to her misery. Henin-Hardenne had been struck down by something that sounded like glandular fever. It was called cytomegalovirus, and when doctors discovered that Justine also had immune system problems, she knew she was in deep trouble. Later Justine admitted: 'It was probably caused by being over-trained. I never stopped, I thought I was a machine, that everything would be fine all the time. Then I realised I had gone too far.'

A burning desire to defend her precious French title led Henin-Hardenne to Roland Garros in May, even though deep down she must have known that her attempt would be futile. Sure enough, she was knocked out in the second round by Tathiana Garbin of Italy, the world number 86. 'It was probably too soon to come back but I had to return one day,' she said sadly.

It was a miracle she had summoned the strength to play at all, because on bad days in early 2004 the virus had incapacitated her completely. Justine had sometimes slept between 14 and 18 hours a day, finding little more energy than was required to keep herself clean and read the odd book. It was the body's way of demanding the rest it would need before beginning a natural fight back. She had always relished a battle, although this particular fight back was proving harder than most. Later she reflected: 'It was another tough time – not just in my career but in my life. But slowly I got better.'

Wimbledon was never a serious possibility after weeks virtually bedridden, followed by false dreams and French failure. But there was something much more crazy she could do for an adrenalin surge, to remind her what it felt like to be alive. In the temporary absence of a body fit enough to compete in big-time tennis, she decided to let gravity do the work for her.

Justine described what happened next. 'After I lost early in the French Open I needed something else because I was thinning down in my career and I wasn't healthy any more, so my husband said: "Let's go skydiving!" I needed something to help me find the adrenalin again, and I found it! We caught the last plane that was going to take the skydivers up at 9.00pm. It was amazing. You feel very, very nervous on the plane. That's maybe what I feel before walking on court, so it's pretty similar. It's a bit crazy. You need to be crazy to do it. Even if you are really scared you should just do it once because you will be really proud of yourself afterwards. Just do it. You'll see how it feels. That's all I can say.'

Justine scared the life out of herself; and at the same time she scared herself back to life. Inspired, she began to look for the next realistic tennis challenge. She focused on an ambition that had captured her imagination for some time, though for most of the year it must have seemed beyond her reach. The Olympic Games were due to take place in Athens later that summer; the most revered sporting tournament of them all was going home to Greece, and it was bound to be a special occasion. Massive as the Olympics were, Justine felt they might offer a less pressurised environment for a recovering tennis player, since her chosen sport wasn't naturally associated with the Games in the public consciousness. Therefore Athens offered her a tantalising adventure in which she really had nothing to lose, and everything to gain.

The ultimate dream was a gold medal, and if that happened no one would be more delighted than Jacques Rogge, the International Olympic Committee President, who also happened to be from Belgium. It wasn't a very realistic target though. The best tennis players would be there, including Venus Williams, the reigning Olympic champion, and Justine had played only two matches in four months. The Olympic schedule demanded that the eventual winner, whoever she may be, would have to play six matches in a week. In short, you had to be supremely fit and very much on top of your game. Justine wasn't fully fit and barely had a game to be on top of that summer. No matter, she decided to go for it.

As soon as she joined up with the 50-odd Belgian athletes who would share the Olympic experience, she felt she had done the right thing. There was a common desire and camaraderie that she wasn't used to in her normal sporting life. She explained later: 'I knew everybody in the Belgian team and being in a group was great because I'm in an individual sport and that's not easy all the time. I'm alone on the court. In Athens I was alone on the court too, but I could hear and feel the whole country behind me.'

That warm feeling of being supported didn't seem to help much when a nervous Henin-Hardenne was broken in her very first game in Athens by the unknown Barbora Strycova; unusually blustery conditions provided an added challenge. But Justine soon settled into her stride, and suddenly realised that she was so happy to be playing again that it really didn't matter how nervous she was. Seventy-five minutes later, her class had shone though, and she had negotiated her first round match 6-3, 6-4.

'I'm probably enjoying my tennis like I never did in the past, because I've been away from the courts a long time,' said Justine afterwards. 'Even if I was nervous, I still have good feelings on court. I finally feel healthy. That's the most important thing.'

Growing in confidence, Justine notched up an even more emphatic victory against Maria Veno-Kabchi of Venezuela in the second round, winning 6-2, 6-1. And by the time she faced Australia's Nicole Pratt in the third, she was playing with some of her old ruthlessness – the 6-1, 6-0 scoreline helping her to conserve some precious energy for the tougher challenges ahead. Perhaps the most fearsome potential obstacle at the quarter-final stage, Venus Williams, was removed from the equation by Mary Pierce of France. Henin-Hardenne was looking sharp and agile by the time she met Pierce, and exposed her opponent's lack of speed around the court with a relatively straightforward 6-4, 6-4 victory.

There was absolutely nothing straightforward about Justine's semi-final against Anastasia Myskina of Russia, a match that went down as one of the most dramatic in Olympic history. It could have been reasonably simple had she held her serve for a 7-5, 6-4 triumph. But Justine squandered the chance to guarantee herself at least a silver medal when she was broken twice in quick succession. Now the contest was all square, each player having taken a set 7-5. The momentum with her, the wiry Russian in the red dress began to play some of the best tennis of her life, and pulverised a shaky Henin to storm into a 5-1 lead. So it was Anastasia's turn to serve for a place in the final; and it was also her turn to take her eye off the ball.

Justine, playing in brilliant white, proceeded to dazzle the Athens crowd with some devil-may-care tennis and started to fight her way out of the corner she was in. Myskina became frustrated, and when she saw her lead reduced to 5-4 she smashed her racket down on the hard surface. It didn't go down too well with the Greek spectators; but when Anastasia lost yet another game, and it quickly sunk in that she had wasted her lead completely, she won everybody's heart. For although she put her hand over her mouth in an attempt to hide her quivering lips, Myskina couldn't disguise her shuddering diaphragm, or indeed the tears pouring down her cheeks as she began to cry with sheer despair.

Even Justine, with her built-in killer instinct, looked stunned as she stared over the net and saw the extraordinary sight of her opponent falling apart emotionally. There was even sympathy in her gaze, and for a good few moments she looked moved by the destruction she had caused in Myskina's soul. Then, as was really her only option, she went about trying to destroy Anastasia some more.

But the tears had changed something, and for a while there was fresh resistance from the highly strung Russian. She even managed to halt the slide to oblivion and won a game during the following minutes, although Justine only tightened her grip on the match and went 7-6 ahead. Pretty soon the pair of them were locked in a rally that would decide Myskina's fate. And Justine's trademark backhand, unleashed with supremely explosive timing, put Anastasia out of her misery. As usual, Henin-Hardenne threw away her racket and buried her head in her hands, scarcely able to believe that she had come back from nowhere, and would now do battle for the gold medal. She almost cried herself, relief and wonder swimming in her eyes at the thought that her tennis magic, the gift she feared destroyed forever by the force of the virus, had returned as before.

As for Anastasia Myskina, some say she never fully recovered from the ordeal. 'If you're 5-1 up you have to finish the match, no matter what,' she said afterwards, and may still be beating herself up about it to this very day.

Justine explained her own, happier demonstration of emotion like this: 'There was big pressure, I haven't slept much in the last few days, but I'm really happy now and I'll recover in time for the final.' And she did, so much so that the showpiece itself was an anti-climax by comparison, at least for everyone except Justine. She took on the French giant, Amelie Mauresmo, and tamed her with a 6-3, 6-3 triumph, the gold medal sealed with a smash.

Carlos Rodriguez leapt up and blew his player a kiss out of both hands. Pierre-Yves was almost sluggish by comparison, though he soon saluted is wife's latest sporting miracle with the enthusiasm it deserved. Tears filled Justine's eyes again, in partial disbelief and sheer joy that her Olympic dream had come true so soon after she had been virtually bedridden.

Her brother Thomas told me later: 'That Olympic gold meant more to her than most people seem to realise, as much as any of her Grand Slam titles.' You could see it in her smile as she wore a crown of laurel leaves and stood highest on the podium, singing her national anthem with glistening pride. Rogge, the Olympic President, was there to see the ceremony just as he had promised. The moment was a piece of perfection. Justine will always cherish the memory, and revealed: 'When I won the Olympic gold in Athens it was one of the best human experiences of my tennis life.'

Her year didn't continue on the high it deserved, because she was knocked out of the US Open by Nadia Petrova in the fourth round, kissing goodbye to her world number one status in the process. Knee and hamstring problems meant she could look forward to a long, hard winter. But after what she had been through that spring, she knew she was lucky just to be dreaming of a long-term return to the highest level. From a burnt-out shell of a woman who could do little more than sleep, she had turned into a courageous Olympian and golden girl. Sporting comebacks don't come much more dramatic than that. The memory of Athens would help sustain her until she could go in search of more glory.

CHAPTER 27
HAT-TRICKS AND ROLLERCOASTERS

JUSTINE WAS LOOKING DOWN THE BARREL OF A GUN again, facing match point at 4-5 in the final set. When Svetlana Kuznetsova was good, she was outstanding, and it seemed unfortunate for Justine that the Russian had hit such a rich vein of form in the round of 16 at the 2005 French Open.

Seeded number 10 for the tournament, Justine had only returned to the tour in March after a total of seven months out with her viral problems and injuries. She had missed the Australian Open with a nagging knee injury and still hadn't regained full fitness. She had battled hard for three hours, despite her ring-rust, but now it looked as though her Roland Garros campaign was over for another year. Then Justine studied the eyes of her opponent, and saw something that gave her hope.

Justine explained later: 'I felt she was nervous when she had that match point. I could see she was afraid to win the match. When you see that in the eyes of your opponent it makes you feel very good.' It is worth considering that remarkable observation for a moment. Justine wasn't playing well, she had been out there for three hours and she was one shot from defeat; but still she felt 'very good'. A warrior's mentality is an extraordinary thing. Needless to say, Henin-Hardenne saved the match point and recovered to beat Svetlana 7-6, 4-6, 7-5.

'It's a kind of miracle that I managed to stay in the match even though I was not able to play by best tennis,' Justine claimed. Some would put it down to sheer force of will, though Kuznetsova put it down to experience. 'I feel like the match was in my hands, I had so many chances. I was dictating the points and I felt much fitter than her. I guess maybe her experience showed in the end.'

The turning point in this match proved something else too: you can have the most powerful game on tour, but to be the best tennis player in the world you have to be able to play mind games like no one else.

Justine tamed the screaming Maria Sharapova 6-4, 6-2 in her quarter-final; and although she wasn't at her ruthless best in her semi-final against Nadia Petrova, she still won comfortably, 6-2, 6-3. Afterwards Justine mused: 'I'm getting a bit tired but I keep winning and that's a good feeling. And if I could have played one more Grand Slam final in my career, it would have been here because this is such a special place for me, with lots of memories.'

The final would be against local favourite Mary Pierce, and there was no tension between them. Justine later admitted: 'Mary is somebody I like very much and respect a lot.' As astonished fans watched Henin-Hardenne break a shell-shocked Mary three times to win the first set 6-1 in 24 minutes, however, it was tempting to wonder what she would have done that day to a player she didn't like or respect. Justine romped away with the second set too, and Pierce double-faulted to go 1-5 down in front of her own fans. When she failed to clear the net after little more than an hour, Mary's humiliation was complete. Justine's 6-1, 6-1 victory was the most one-sided demolition Paris had seen since her heroine, Steffi Graf, had thrashed Natasha Zvereva back in 1988.

Henin-Hardenne's smile was so radiant it threatened to burn away the clouds still hanging over Roland Garros. She said: 'There are no words to describe this moment because I have lived through some very difficult times in the last year. It is so emotional for me and fills me with happiness. I think I am enjoying my tennis more now than before my illness. Every ball I hit, it's with my heart.' There was still no acknowledgement of her father, although doubtless her late mother continued to inspire her. Above all, however, Justine's second French Open triumph appeared to have been born in the frightened eyes of Svetlana Kuznetsova, as she squandered that inviting match point.

By the time Justine went in search of a Roland Garros hat-trick in 2006, her conduct was already steeped in controversy. She had suffered adverse publicity before, when sporting purists had shaken their heads at the manner of victory against Serena Williams in Paris, 2003, and Kim Clijsters in Melbourne, 2004. This time she had attracted criticism in Melbourne again, though for the way she had lost not won. Amelie Mauresmo had pulverised Justine 6-1 in the first set of their Australian Open final, and was also winning the second set when Henin-Hardenne called in the trainer.

To spectators it seemed surprising because Justine had

been showing no obvious signs of distress other than a natural frustration at being played off the court. It later emerged, however, that she had woken at 3.30am with a terrible burning sensation in her stomach. She had taken anti-inflammatory medication for a sore shoulder, and that appeared to have caused an adverse reaction. Rather than pull out of the final, which she had considered doing early that morning, Justine had decided to play and see how she went. Now it was perfectly obvious she was going to lose, but instead of going through the motions and giving Mauresmo her deserved moment of triumph, Henin-Hardenne packed her bags at 6-1, 2-0 and called it a day.

Perhaps Justine could sense that the knives were out for her when she reached the press conference, because she soon leaned forward and appeared to be crying, although she tried to cover her face with her hands. This expression of distress from the toughest lady in tennis was one of the most unusual sights the tour had seen in recent times. 'I was playing the best tennis of my career, I had a chance to get another big title and I really wanted it,' she admitted through her tears. 'That it ends like this is difficult.'

But the hardened reporters weren't about to let her off the hook quite so easily; they still didn't see why it had ended so suddenly, and accused her of an ungracious exit. 'Everyone has the right to think that, but it's my health,' insisted Justine. 'When you're on court, and you suffer a lot, and you feel you don't have anything to give, it's pretty hard to stay on the court. I have no regrets about the decision I took.'

Perhaps we should all have known what would happen at Roland Garros, because an angry Justin Henin-Hardenne arrived at her favourite tournament with a point to prove.

She raced around the clay courts in what she calls her 'garden' in a controlled rage, and she didn't drop a set or even need a tie-break on her way to the final. Waiting for her in the showpiece was the familiar face of Svetlana Kuznetsova, who was learning guile to go with her power and looked impressive. What she didn't have, however, was her opponent's motivation, and Justine outgunned her hard-hitting opponent 6-4, 6-4, pausing only for a Mexican Wave to subside before she served successfully for the match.

'I didn't think about what happened in Australia during today's final, but it had been a motivation,' Justine admitted. 'I wanted to finish a Grand Slam final differently. By a victory, of course, but also with me being able to fight on court. And that's what happened. I'm very happy about that.' It seemed that the chink in Justine's armour had been repaired, her fearsome image as the tour's top fighter restored. And now she had three victories at Roland Garros under her belt, an incredible achievement given that she had feared her career was over just two years earlier.

When she spoke to the assembled media after one of the most devastating French Open campaigns on record, Justine's achievement clearly hadn't quite sunk in. It was becoming a habit to honour her mother by winning this particular crown, but that didn't make each new triumph any easier. Justine was becoming a tennis legend, people were starting to call her the finest clay court player of her generation. Did she have the focus to keep on winning in Paris after collecting an amazing three singles titles in four years? Time would tell, but she didn't have the kind of personality that led you to believe she would ever ease up in her campaign to become the greatest female player Roland Garros had ever seen.

'Everything I live is very intense,' she explained. 'In my career, in my life, in my relationship, all the time it's very intense. Right now I can't find the words to describe this third win here, it's too early. But I know when you win the same tournament three times, it probably means a lot. It's very tough to win here.'

Despite being crowned queen of Roland Garros yet again, Henin-Hardenne couldn't shake off the controversy surrounding the Mauresmo final in Australia. And when the same two players reached the final of Wimbledon that year, the sense of anticipation was intense. Would Justine take revenge there for the way she had been criticised? (Mauresmo hadn't exactly diffused the situation in Melbourne when she had said of Justine: 'If she hadn't stopped, people would have been talking about the fact that she played a bad match. It's just the way it goes, but my joy is still there. I was ready to die on court today . . .') Or was Amelie's anger at having been denied her moment of triumph in Melbourne still strong enough to ensure that she won again, this time with Henin-Hardenne waiting dutifully on the other side of the net to salute her superiority?

Justine seemed in killer form right from the start, taking the first set by an emphatic 6-2. It was five years since she had played her first final at the All England Club, and the memories of losing her grandfather that day were still vivid. At last it looked as though she was doing justice to herself in England, and marking the tragedy that had befallen Georges Rosiere with a Wimbledon victory he would have loved. But then the exertions of a full fortnight at Roland Garros, combined with the effort expended in staying the course for another fortnight in London's SW19, seemed to catch up with Justine. She appeared to take her foot off the pedal, perhaps led astray by fatigue and the loss of concentration it can cause.

Mauresmo, whose big-match temperament had been questioned until that very year, stormed back to take the second set 6-3. Justine didn't have the energy to turn the tide, and Amelie claimed her first Wimbledon title by closing out the final set 6-4. A heartbroken Henin-Hardenne was asked whether it is unrealistic to expect to win Wimbledon just a few weeks after winning Roland Garros. 'Oh, I was pretty close to it,' she replied wistfully. 'So it means it is possible. I was just a set from that. You know, it turned away.'

When Justine Henin-Hardenne reached the last two of the US Open a few weeks later, it meant she had earned herself a place in the final of every Grand Slam event that year, an extraordinary achievement in itself. But finals are no place to be if you don't win them, and the bitter taste of defeat wasn't any easier to bear than it had been at Wimbledon. Maria Sharapova was her conqueror, 6-4, 6-4, and Henin-Hardenne's Grand Slam statistics were both impressive and disappointing at the same time. Four finals, three defeats; not the sort of win-lose ratio she was used to, though it left her in a straight fight to become world number one.

In November, there was one last chance to end the year on a high, at the WTA Championship in Madrid. The battle for world supremacy would finish there for another season, and a long struggle was still very much in the balance. Both Sharapova and Justine had the chance to be crowned queen of tennis for 2006, Mauresmo having fallen behind. As it turned out, the much-anticipated showdown between Maria and Justine came in the semi-final.

Maria was favourite after her US success, especially since she had built up an impressive record of 19 straight wins. A 20th victory would give her the number one spot, and leave a frustrated Justine reflecting on a year largely spent playing bridesmaid at the big occasions. The thought of playing second fiddle yet again was so unbearable that it gave the underdog an edge few had foreseen.

Against the odds, Henin-Hardenne fought ferociously to shatter Sharapova's winning run and claim end-of-year supremacy for herself. The 6-2, 7-6 victory meant everything to Justine, not least an escape from the torment a natural-born-winner would have felt going into the Christmas break as the nearly-girl. At the end of the rollercoaster ride that 2006 had given her, Justine knew she had taken the blows, learned from the near misses and hit back to clamber over her rivals and regain the top spot.

'She deserves it,' said Maria graciously. 'She was the most consistent player all year round.'

Justine couldn't celebrate yet though, because she had unfinished business in the final. Waiting there was her nemesis, Mauresmo, and no matter how they might try to play it down, this was a grudge match. Following the US Open Henin-Hardenne had been out for two months with a muscle tear, and despite her obvious frustration, the rest appeared to have served her well. She wasn't feeling ill or jaded, as she had been for her previous big clashes against Mauresmo in Melbourne and London – just very aggressive. Playing in a white cap, turquoise top and black shorts, a liberated Justine thrilled the Madrid crowd with a scintillating display of tennis, full of versatility and ruthlessness.

With irresistible stroke-play, she crafted winners from all

angles and bombarded Mauresmo from start to finish. Revenge was sweet. The 6-4, 6-3 scoreline didn't tell the full story of Justine's quality, particularly as the match reached its climax, though she made sure her master class was recognised afterwards.

'I think I just played amazing tennis in the last three games,' said Henin-Hardenne. 'I really wanted this victory and I have proved some things to myself right at the end of the season. I'm number one, so today is as good as winning a Grand Slam. I'm just so happy now, I can't explain it.'

That happiness, however, was to be short-lived.

CHAPTER 28
THE SPLIT

PROFESSIONALLY, LIFE COULD HARDLY HAVE BEEN BETTER for the golden girl. Henin-Hardenne realised with some satisfaction that she had become the first player to reach all four Grand Slam finals and the WTA final in the same year since her heroine, Steffi Graf, had achieved the feat in 1993. Justine was only the fifth player ever to do so. But now that the serious tennis was over for a while, she was left to reflect upon the state of her relationship with her husband Pierre-Yves.

Justine had already been finding the supposed permanence of marriage a difficult concept to cope with, according to her coach Carlos Rodriguez. When the Argentinian was interviewed towards the end of 2006, the story he recounted suggested that some of the Henin-Hardenne romance had faded. Rodriguez said: 'She revealed to me something incredible she had told Pierre-Yves – "I cannot come to terms with the idea that I'll always be married to you. Now we are, tomorrow who knows? That's the way we'll go to the end."'

Living in the present was one way to sustain the union, but it would take a lot more than that. Alphonse Henin,

Justine's paternal grandfather, who had been married to her grandmother Jeanne for more than 60 years, had a saying: 'Love is blind. Marriage opens the eyes.' It was how you reacted when reality hit home that mattered; and if a marriage was going to survive beyond the initial, magical phase, then it helped if you could see that you still had plenty in common as a couple, so that you could enjoy less exciting times together.

Christmas and New Year proved a rude awakening for Justine, whose focus on her home life had, by her own admission, become somewhat blurred due to the extraordinary dedication she had shown to her tennis career. Later, looking back on her time with Pierre-Yves, she admitted: 'It's really tough to be involved one hundred per cent in your marriage and also to be involved one hundred per cent in your career. My marriage was important because I needed to find a lot of stability and a lot of security, which I got. But sometimes you don't grow up at the same – with the same needs, and you don't want the same things.'

Justine and Pierre-Yves had met when she was only 16, and in many ways still a child. He had promoted her independence, aided her march into adulthood, and been good for her tennis while the romance lasted. But by 24 she was a grown woman, respected and wealthy; she had matured fast and she was in a natural position to call the shots. In short, she had blossomed and times had changed.

Carlos had recently defended his own decision to encourage Justine to marry, when originally asked for his advice in 2001; but he was at pains to point out that he wouldn't necessarily have been so encouraging had he been asked the same question in 2006. He explained: 'Everyone was against her marriage. But one year after, she became number one in the world. It was highly important to know the context. If 10 people ask me for advice, I wouldn't tell them to marry, except for her in that very moment, it seemed right. Five years later, I don't know what I would have told her.'

Five years later, to the outsider at least, there seemed to be little balance of power between Henin, the multi-millionairess sporting superstar, and Hardenne, who appeared to dislike the spotlight. Though again this wasn't necessarily anyone's fault, the imbalance was potentially damaging, because without true equilibrium any marriage is likely to come under severe strain. If one partner feels she or he has outgrown the other, then a previously happy union is probably doomed.

By the time the world welcomed in 2007, Justine had faced facts. Her marriage, for which she had left her own family behind, was over. There was no going back, and never again would she play under the name Henin-Hardenne. The life she had imagined beyond tennis with Pierre-Yves, the future she had once talked about so enthusiastically, would never become a reality. The dream had died, it was the end of an era. The decision to end a marriage is difficult and very personal, and it would be wrong to enter into specifics or to apportion blame. What mattered was Justine's grim realisation that Pierre-Yves wasn't the man for her after all. The reality was no less shocking or upsetting for her than it was for him.

She admitted: 'I didn't know if I was going to be able to overcome these problems.' Disorientated, she announced her withdrawal from the Australian Open in the first week of January, and almost immediately the split became public knowledge. A certain irony lay in the timing; only when the marriage was over did Justine finally feel compelled to take an extended break from the constant, corrosive grind of the circuit.

It is no secret that Pierre-Yves found it difficult to be seen following his wife around the world on the WTA tour, sometimes struggling to find a suitable professional role to play within her entourage. There is only so long that any self-respecting man will put up with a general feeling of not quite belonging in a very incestuous and self-absorbed world, however much that man might want to do the right thing by his wife. The circuit is only glamorous for those at the centre of attention, or at least with an important job to do within that world. Otherwise the goldfish bowl can seem very restricting and irksome. What realistic chance did the young couple have of sustaining their love affair under these unnatural conditions, when even Justine admitted: 'The tour is not real life.'?

Alphonse Henin used to say that a simple secret lay behind a husband's ability to survive in a marriage. 'Always do what your wife tells you to do.' It is an amusing line, but a hard rule to follow; especially if you are a young man seeking to preserve your own identity and sense of independence while under constant scrutiny in the bubble of a high-profile relationship.

Would that relationship have had a better chance of survival had Pierre-Yves heeded the advice of Justine's father Jose back in 1999, and began as early as possible the process of building his own career, in order to give himself a separate life and identity from the start, away from Justine's tennis? Did Pierre-Yves realise the importance of this too late? It is impossible to say, though there seems to be an irony in Pierre-Yves' apparent refusal to give Jose's suggestions due respect all those years earlier.

Jose, however, certainly wasn't gloating when he told me some months after the separation: 'Now Pierre-Yves understands some of what I had to go through when Justine walked out of my life, and all the changes you have to make to your social life on top of everything else. But I wish him well, I really do, I hope he will be OK, not least because if Justine knows that Pierre-Yves is alright, I think it will be better for her happiness too.'

When the dust finally settles, Pierre-Yves may be able to look back with fondness on the skydiving, his selfless tears of joy as Justine first won Roland Garros, and the thrill of being part of a young couple who were, in many ways, taking on the world together. The question in the aftermath of the split, when the dust still clouded everything, was to what extent Justine might retain the appetite to take on the tennis world alone. Some of those in rival camps were never in any doubt about her ability to bounce back with her strength undiminished. Richard Williams, father of Venus and Serena, told me: 'I like Justine, she is one tough lady. If something gets in the way, she moves it right out of the way. She even moved her husband out of the way.'

But that was hardly a fair reading of the situation, and Justine was certainly feeling extremely fragile at the start of 2007. With the prospect of divorce looming large, she was sufficiently scared in January to wonder whether she might no longer be capable of concentrating on her tennis. 'I think divorce is tough for everyone,' she said looking back on those dark weeks. 'Especially when you have to compete in front of 20,000 people and your mind is somewhere else.' So her rivals played the Australian Open without her, and some people continued to wonder whether Justine Henin would ever be quite the same player again.

The idea of returning to the circuit was daunting; and when she risked being consumed by self-doubt, her coach, Carlos Rodriguez, was a huge source of strength to her, whatever the time of day or night. Justine explained: 'We are so close. If I have a problem at three in the morning, I can call him and he will be there for me, and respect has been the key between the two of us, it has been the word.'

Carlos helped to convince Justine that there would be a happy life waiting for her after Pierre-Yves, on and off the tennis court, as long as they took her recovery from her fresh personal trauma slowly. As the weeks passed, one door closed and another opened.

CHAPTER 29
A CRASH-COURSE IN SALADS

THERE WERE MANY TIMES WHEN IT WAS HARD FOR Justine to see the light at the end of the tunnel, and when the split from Pierre-Yves appeared to have sent her career spinning all the way back to square one. She knew she could never hope to get over her personal crisis until she had proved she could still function professionally. Bravely, she picked up her tennis racket and prepared to take her first tentative steps out onto court, using her old name. She revealed later: 'I tried to keep focused on my tennis and to rebuild my confidence. It was important to keep working, to keep busy. When I look back to the way I felt in January and when I came back to competition again, it felt like I had to start my career all over again.'

Her sport released Justine from her pain, albeit temporarily, and her tennis skills didn't desert her just because she had become plain old Henin again, instead of the Grand Slam title-winning Henin-Hardenne. Although mentally there was still a considerable way to go, she knew she had taken the hardest step as soon as she saw a competitive opponent waiting on the other side of the net. So the tournament she played in Paris in February was regarded as a personal triumph, even though she didn't win a trophy.

The prestigious Laureus Sports Awards in Barcelona provided a timely boost to her confidence, and reinforced her standing as one of the great sportswomen of her era. Everyone seemed glad to see that her life was back on track, and that one of the game's great stars hadn't been lost to tennis entirely. As soon as she could focus with her customary sharpness again – and that would only be a matter of time – the trophies would surely come thick and fast, just as they had done before.

However, events in Justine's native Belgium turned her life upside down again. A text from her sister Sarah broke the dreadful news of a car crash involving her brother, David. The thought of another death in the Henin family, after all they had been through, was almost too much for her to bear. Perhaps it was just as well that she was stranded in another country and spared the details of David's horrific accident. But would she leave her relationship with her brother unresolved, or fly to his bedside and risk rejection?

Although it was touch and go for a while, David survived to tell the tale of what had happened to him. It wasn't easy to live it all again in his mind, and it was obvious he would only do so in his own time. We met up in October 2007 in Belgium, and he agreed to describe in painful detail how a typical spring night in a fun city suddenly went terribly wrong. Fittingly, perhaps, the venue for the interview was the restaurant he had just opened in Liege, 'Le Saint Paul Gourmand'. It is a poignant symbol of survival, because the fact that he was able to pursue any kind of professional dream so soon, let alone run his own restaurant, was a minor miracle considering the injuries he sustained. Lunchtime access to David's first-floor tables is gained through the butcher's shop below, while for dinner his customers enter through the restaurant kitchens; nothing in the Henin family is ever straightforward. But the more you get to know the survivors in a group of people regularly hit by tragedy, the more you marvel at their resilience.

When David recounted the horrors of his accident in late March 2007, it became clear that the memories were still relatively raw and traumatic. The 34-year-old told me: 'On that particular night back in March I had been working quite late in the bar belonging to our brother Thomas, which is situated just around the corner here in Saint Paul. Before midnight I left to go back to my father Jose's house in the town of Marche-en-Famenne, because that's where I was staying at the time.'

Climbing into his Volkswagen Passat, David left behind Saint Paul, with its beggars, buskers and Gothic Cathedral, most notable perhaps for the extraordinary location of the 'Pissoir' or public, open-air urinal which allows the citizens of Liege to relieve themselves almost up against a sacred wall of the dear old building itself. He took a familiar route to climb up out of Liege, and struggled to keep his eyes open during the tedious, 45-minute drive south. Then it happened. David recalled: 'I was only about three kilometres from the house when I crashed into a lamppost. I had fallen asleep at the wheel.'

And the wheel had a cruel way of letting Justine's brother know what he had done. With a visible wince he explained: 'The steering wheel smashed into my ribs and broke seven of them – six on the left-hand side and one on the other side. The biggest problem was that one of those broken ribs had punctured a big hole in my lung, about five centimetres from my heart.' (At this point in the interview David made a hole using his forefinger and thumb which was large enough to slide a snooker cue through.) 'It was hard to breathe and there was so much, so much pain.'

Since the seductive power of sleep had caused the problem in the first place, you might have thought that another of the body's natural defence mechanisms – the ability to switch off when confronted with excruciating pain – would have ensured a merciful, fresh loss of consciousness. But that mechanism didn't kick in at all, so he had to sit there under that now-distorted lamppost, his steering wheel almost embedded in his torso.

David added: 'I remember everything. I was fully conscious and in agony as I waited for the emergency services to arrive. They got me out and took me to hospital in Marche. That night my father brought my son Noah to hospital, and my sister Sarah was there too.' He didn't know whether this was his last chance to say goodbye to his loved ones. No one knew if he would survive, and so Sarah contacted Justine to tell her what had happened. The tennis star hadn't spoken to her brother for seven years, and now it appeared that it might be too late to repair the rift.

Jose took up the story: 'The results of the initial X-rays and scans came back, and the doctors were horrified to see how much damage one of his broken ribs had done as it punctured that big hole in David's lung. If he had stayed in the hospital in Marche he would have died.' Fortunately everyone realised what had to be done. David remembered: 'I was still awake the next morning when they strapped me up as tightly as they could and put me in a helicopter to fly me back to Liege. I was taken to the Centre Hospitalier Universitaire. At that point I was still aware of everything that was happening to me, though of course I was finding it hard to breathe. The pain was so great that I just wanted to pass out, but it wasn't happening.'

Once he was in intensive care in Liege, however, the doctors put David out of his misery. Jose explained: 'The doctors in Liege put David in a coma, they induced it because they thought it would offer him the best chance to undergo and survive the operation he needed. But I thought I was going to lose my son. He was somewhere between life and death at that point.' David's wife Leila and his younger brother Thomas rushed to the hospital in Liege and stayed close to him in his hour of need. But hours began to turn into days. 'I stayed in that coma for two days in all,' David told me, as calmly as he could.

And during those two days Justine was still faced with an agonising choice. She could stay away, remembering how hurt she had felt back in 1999 when David, Thomas and their father Jose had apparently failed to accept her future husband Pierre-Yves; or she could take David's accident as a sign that it was time to forget the past and move on. She knew that others who were now far closer to David would be there, offering all the support he needed. Would it really make a positive difference if she tried to walk back into his life at such a sensitive time? Didn't he have enough to deal with already?

Two days passed and David woke up, though he wasn't out of danger yet. 'Breathing was still very difficult, which is what made the surprise so important,' he claimed later. And this is how David described the 'surprise'. 'Just after I came out of the coma, at about 8.00pm one evening, my sister Sarah came in with her boyfriend Louis and my brother Thomas. And then there was Justine. I didn't know she was coming and it was the first time we had been together for seven years. It was emotional, so very powerful because we had been so long apart. I don't remember what was said, or even if we spoke. All I know is that we were both crying.'

Justine Henin, the ice-maiden of world tennis, had shown herself to be only human, and had decided that enough was enough, at least where David and their brother Thomas were concerned. 'I had taken the accident as a sign,' admitted Justine later. And, deep down, she had been open to such a sign for some time. David explained: 'Justine, I later learned, had been prepared to see us for some months, ever since the break-up with Pierre-Yves. But the accident seemed to her a good time to do it, even though it was a dramatic moment to choose.' In November 2007 Justine confirmed to the *Sunday Times* of London: 'David was conscious when I arrived and Thomas was sitting by his bed. It was the first time I had seen them for seven years and we all just started crying.'

Thomas, who can be intense or fun-loving depending on the moment, had publicly disowned Justine three years earlier. Now they too were brother and sister again. All four siblings were together as adults for the first time. And yet even in that moment of heart-wrenching drama, there was something – or rather someone – missing. David confirmed: 'My father wasn't there when I met Justine. He came in again the following morning with Leila, my wife. Jose and Justine never got to see each other in that hospital.'

But Jose, who had endured seven tortuous years without Justine, heard something interesting from his other children when next they spoke. He recalled: 'Apparently Justine was looking around all the time in that hospital, as though she was expecting me to come in. But I had already decided that it was better for me to stay away and give her that opportunity to see her brothers again, without me getting in the way of everything.'

And so as Justine left the hospital that day, delighted at least that David had found the long, hard road to recovery, something else was on her mind; something unresolved and deeply worrying to her. Jose later revealed what Justine had said as she drove away from that Liege hospital with her sister Sarah. 'Justine turned to her sister and asked her straight: "Does Papa still love me?"

Sarah looked Justine in the eye. "Why don't you call him and ask him yourself?"'

Justine hesitated. One of the toughest people in world sport – male or female – was scared.

The future unity of the Henin family hung in the balance. There was just one more piece of ice-breaking to complete if the feud was to be well and truly consigned to history. The two most stubborn members of that family, Justine and Jose, the daughter and father who had clashed with such devastating consequences, both waited nervously, full of apprehension at the thought of fresh contact. Both feared it, both wanted it. But who would make the first move? In a way the answer was neither. Typically, it was the unsung heroine of the Henin family, the one person who had never given up hope that peace might one day break out, who provided the final push.

As Justine and Sarah Henin dined together that evening, and the question of Jose's love remained unresolved, the tennis star's little sister kept up the gentle pressure. Then she dialled Jose's number and handed her big sister the phone. Jose recalled the brief, nervous exchange, its simplicity almost making a mockery of the long, painful years of miscommunication. 'Justine said: "Hi Papa, how are you, will you come out to lunch?" I agreed. The venue was to be my sister Genevieve's restaurant in Han-sur-Lesse.'

In so few words, wounded pride was swallowed on both sides. Father and daughter had taken a giant preliminary step, and punctured holes in their seemingly interminable conflict. What had been the secret? Just enough courtesy to fill 10 tricky seconds.

Neither Justine nor Jose really knew how the meeting would go until it took place a couple of days later. Even so, Justine had a good feeling about it. She recalled later: 'For a few years I was scared to see my daddy again. Scared about what I would feel, but that day when I was driving to see him, I was just so happy.' She arrived first, so it was Jose who had to make the big entrance. 'He had changed a lot, he had put on weight,' Justine remembered thinking. Jose, of course, knew what his daughter looked like these days, along with many millions of others. Words were hard to come by at first. He recalled: 'I went in and said "hello" to Justine and she said "hello" to me. But nothing much was said.'

One word each didn't seem like very generous compensation for seven years of angry silence. There was no warm embrace; no tears of joy were shed to compare with those shared spontaneously by the siblings in that Liege hospital a day or two earlier. For a few anxious moments, the entire reconciliation seemed to hang in the balance, and it appeared that much would depend on the table plan for the meal itself.

Jose remembered: 'When we all sat down to eat, Justine was placed next to me. It was the first time I had been to Genevieve's restaurant, and I was feasting my eyes on the menu. Justine turned to me and said: 'Don't even bother to use your eyes looking at that. It has already been decided. You're having a salad.'

Jose looked at Justine. His daughter looked at him right back. And smiles spread across their faces. 'It was harsh but funny and it really broke the ice and relaxed us. From that moment on we talked as though we had never been apart.' Justine felt the same way. 'We were both so happy. After two minutes it was as if we had been together the day before.'

So David had come out of his coma, Jose had emerged from a personal nightmare, and Justine had survived the emotional impact of her marriage break-up. Sarah and Thomas had their sister back after all those years of pain, Alphonse and Jeanne had their granddaughter, and Jean-Paul and Jean-Marie had their niece. What could put the icing on the cake, or more appropriately the dressing on the salad? Well, there was always Roland Garros . . .

CHAPTER 30
ONE FOR PAPA

NERVOUSLY, JUSTINE'S SURVIVING SIBLINGS ASKED IF THEY would be disturbing her by coming to the 2007 French Open. It wasn't just Thomas and Sarah who were keen to watch her at Roland Garros. Incredibly, David wanted to go too, even though his broken bones had barely healed. Justine said they would be welcome, something she had never done before during any of her Grand Slam campaigns. More than that, she invited them to sit in the Tribune des Joueurs, the seats reserved for the players' special guests, the sacred area where Justine had promised her mother, Francoise, she would one day sit.

Ordinarily her father, Jose, would have loved to be there too. Wisely, however, he stayed at home, knowing that it was too early for him to be taking such complicated steps. The temptation to try to join in the party, after all those years of feeling ignored, must have been strong. But he knew that tennis had torn the family apart, and was determined that it wouldn't be allowed to do so again. He had to give Justine the chance to rebuild her relationship with him away from her place of work. Even towards the end of 2007, Justine admitted: 'I don't think I'm ready yet to have him watch me at a tournament – that would be too emotional – and I think he understands. He was always involved in my career, but he has to understand that I don't need him as a coach; I want to be his daughter; I need him as a dad.'

Jose was reading his daughter loud and clear. 'Justine and I see each other all the time now,' he told me that spring. 'But we have a new rule. She only has one father – me. And she only has one coach – Carlos. I don't want to go to her matches because we have to take things slowly, one step at a time. I would rather she does well without me than loses because I am there, having felt some kind of pressure.'

Jose watched all the matches on television as usual, but there was a difference this time. The young woman darting about on his screen was his daughter, Justine, someone he had spoken to just a few hours earlier; not the stranger in the same body that had been so successful and so uncommunicative in years gone by. And after many of her victories in this, her favourite tournament, Justine was quick to call her father so that she could hear his happy reaction to her latest exploits. Jose would tell her that he was proud of her, and not just because of her tennis. He admired the way she was conducting herself as a person too. In fact they would speak only briefly of tennis, and then move onto another topic. They developed their own formula and it worked. He gave her a father's love, and that's what she wanted.

When Justine reached the final, beating Serena Williams and Jelena Jankovic along the way, all the surviving Henin siblings were there. Sure enough, David had kept his promise to attend, despite the discomfort it must have caused him. He had supported Justine in the middle of the night when she played in Australia, even though she had virtually disowned him during the long feud. So the small matter of seven broken ribs, a punctured lung and a recent coma wasn't going to keep him away, not when he had finally received an invitation to see her play a Grand Slam final in the flesh.

Was it hard for him to forgive her for the years of pain? 'It's not about forgiving,' he told me later. 'The past is the past and I have no problem with the past. Life is beginning now. I saw Justine playing mini-golf with Sarah and my son Noah soon after I got out of hospital. I played too and as we did so we laughed so much it hurt, and I just felt lucky to be alive. When Justine comes to Liege, my son Noah often stays in the hotel with her. Other times she will come to eat a barbecue with us at my wife's house, enjoying the simple things in life and the company of her relatives.'

Against that happy backdrop David took his seat at Roland Garros, next to Louis, Sarah's long-standing fiancé. Thomas, who sat the other side of Sarah, had his daughter Kiara close by, and one day she would be able to tell people she had been at the big match. It was a truly poignant scene, because Kiara was six weeks old at the time; precisely the age at which Thomas' son Emilien had died so tragically due to respiratory problems six years earlier. Justine had wounded Thomas deeply by not attending his baby's funeral back in 2001, but they both knew that she couldn't change anything now. He had faced his pain without her, and in time he had carved out a new life for himself. Thomas and Vanessa had split up, he had found happiness with a new partner, and Kiara had arrived a matter of days after David had so nearly died.

As she warmed up, Justine was aware of who was watching from the Tribune des Joueurs, and knew how lucky she was that her family were still prepared to show her so much love and support. Feeling that love from just a few feet away, she began one more Roland Garros final, knowing this one was like no other. Perhaps it was too much to ask her to seal this symbolic moment of reconciliation with a third successive Roland Garros triumph, a fourth French Open in five years. The opening moments of the final suggested that Justine's emotions might be getting the better of her.

Ana Ivanovic, the teenager Serb with the model looks and a forehand to die for, began like she meant business. In an opening game predicted by nobody, she broke the champion with the help of two of those blockbuster forehands. Keeping the pressure on, she cruised to 40-0 on her own service, and suddenly a major shock was in the air.

Then it happened. Ana had trouble with her ball toss on the next serve, and looked embarrassed. Had her amazing start suddenly sunk in, or had it crossed her mind that millions of expectant fans were now waiting for her to continue in the same vein? Whatever it was, Ana's self-belief simply evaporated and she allowed the woman on the other side of the net, who was rapidly becoming a legend, to overwhelm her. Seeing her opponent apparently terrified of taking the lead, Justine went to work with all the ruthlessness that had been missing at the start. Not only did Henin break back, albeit with the help of a net-cord; she didn't allow the newcomer to take another game until the match was all but won.

At many changeovers, Justine, in a bright pink top and white cap, took out a piece of paper and read it. Perhaps

Ivanovic was intimidated by this tactic too. But the winner revealed later that most of the messages had simply stated the blindingly obvious. 'You are the best. Run, run, run,' read one.

Simple self-belief carried the day; David, Thomas and Sarah cheered from the stand as their sister put on an exhibition of devastating quality. The contest, if it could still be called that, became little more than a celebration of their family reunion, and the Henins wouldn't have wanted it any other way. After 65 minutes Justine attacked the net and dispatched a forehand volley to make more history. She had done it, and looked up at her brothers and sisters to see if they were feeling what she was.

The siblings were up on their feet, united in the sort of profound joy that needs no dramatic expression. The win itself hadn't caused that joy, merely enhanced it handsomely. Thomas blew a quiet kiss and waved, as a warm, effortless smile played on his face. There was nothing showy about his reaction at all, every gesture was beautifully understated. There was an understanding between the two that didn't need the theatre of the moment.

Sarah, who had never given up dreaming of a family reunion, and had probably done most to bring it about, managed to look both glamorous and serene. She had turned from insecure girl to confident young woman during the years of the feud, and there was a quiet class about the way she gently applauded her sister, with her handsome fiancé Louis at her side. In a cool black dress, her sunglasses pressed against her hair like a band, and a distinctive long necklace completing the look, Sarah oozed charisma without even trying. Like Thomas, her happiness seemed deep, rich and steady, something to be savoured.

Those with less experience of life might have been overcome by the moment of victory. To the Henin family, this was just sport, even if it was very satisfying sport. Justine's latest triumph was the icing on the cake, but it was the family that really mattered.

David was on his feet applauding at the end of the row, almost out of the snapshot. The lovable man whose brush with death had provided the catalyst for the reunion appeared to have been overlooked by TV cameramen, though not by Justine. Her warm gaze was for David as much as for the others, and the fact that he was able to stand there clapping with the rest of them seemed nothing short of miraculous to those who knew what he had been through only a few short weeks earlier. For David, this was just another wonderful moment to enjoy in a life he now appreciated like never before.

Justine sat on her chair near the umpire, pointed at her family and waved. There was something very different about her smile in her moment of victory this time around. No longer was she trying to chase joy, it was simply there, beaming out of her from the inside. Life held sway over death that day. It was almost as if the journey to self-discovery was over. There was a wisdom born of experience in the understanding she shared with her brothers and sister. The win was a gift to them, and it must have been a relief for Justine to know that she could still claim a Grand Slam with some of her inner rage removed. But it appeared that Justine had realised something about sport too, that it could be more than a means of hitting back at the bad things that had happened to her. Surviving family was just as important as those who had passed away, and when you realised that, you could enjoy your sport even more, and see the pleasure it brought to the faces of the living.

Of course, Justine still pointed both forefingers towards the sky, saluting, reaching out to her mother in thanks. That would never change, it was a bond which would always drive her on. But now there was a family happiness she could see with her own eyes, in the faces of those who remained. And she knew that no one would have been happier than her mother to see the surviving children back together again.

This may have been a new, more satisfying kind of win, but the victory also completed a remarkable hat-trick. Three successive French titles was a feat that hadn't been achieved since the days of Monica Seles in her prime. And incredibly, Justine's 6-1, 6-2 triumph made it 35 straight sets at the tournament she loved best, a dominance that confirmed Henin as the finest clay-courter of her generation by a distance. The legendary Martina Navratilova said afterwards: 'The whole tournament, she was just astonishingly good. She just kept getting better and better. She's the best clay-court player by far.'

The victory speech was always going to be a family affair. Addressing her late mother Francoise, Justine said: 'Thank you to my protector in Heaven, you are with me always. You are always in my heart.' Looking up to her brothers and sister, she added: 'I dedicate this win to my family. I missed you. I love you with all my heart.' Later she explained: 'I looked at them and, just looking at each other, we understood a lot of things.'

But back on court Justine spoke again, and did something for the first time. 'Merci Papa,' she said. 'Thank you daddy, watching back home on television.' Just a few words of simple acknowledgement; but for those of us who knew what Jose had been through all those years, this was by far the most moving moment of all. It was the first time she had publicly recognised his existence at any of her Grand Slam triumphs, and this was her sixth. He did't need to be there to appreciate the gesture, he heard it the moment she said it. Even so, Justine called her father as soon as she left the court, and it was hard for both of them to hold back the tears.

In the players' hospitality area, David held an impromptu press conference, privately worrying that his English would not stand up to the rigorous test. He needn't have been concerned. They actually told him he was speaking too fast. 'We Henins do everything too fast,' he laughed. 'Speak fast, eat fast . . . win fast.' Although winning fast was obviously good, David reckoned that recently Justine had also learned to savour everything in her life while it lasted. 'I look at her this year and see she is laughing, smiling, and taking pleasure in what she does.' Thinking back perhaps to Melbourne 2004, David recalled: 'I used to see her on TV and she did not always look too happy.' He told reporters about his reunion with Justine in the hospital. 'It was very moving and very, very powerful,' he explained. 'It had been too long.'

Justine knew it had been too long as well. 'It's been a huge step in my life the last few months,' she said. 'I was very glad I could give my family this victory, because everyone suffered a lot from the situation in the last few years. And today, finally, we are united in this joy, and we can share this moment.' Later she added: 'I also thought a lot about my mum who would be so proud and happy to see her family together again, a strong family.'

When David had given Justine another cautious hug, protecting his fragile rib cage as he did so, he headed back across the border to Belgium, and Justine continued to embrace those who remained from her family party. Reflecting on her astonishing success, she said: 'I've been a little bit surprised, because it has been hard for me, everything I lived in the last few months, the ups and downs, good things and bad things. And then I realised that it's life. Life is ups and downs, and you have to accept it.'

No one did ups and downs like Justine Henin. And these moments were about as perfect as life could offer. Her brother Thomas passed Justine her six-week-old niece, Kiara, and she cradled the baby lovingly. Justine Henin had come a long way.

CHAPTER 31
LITTLE BOYS AND LITTLE GIRLS

WE STOOD IN THE DRIZZLE AT WIMBLEDON, THOMAS Henin and I, sinking bottles of beer at an unhealthy rate to help us get over the shock. It was only a few short weeks since the triumph of Roland Garros, and now there was sporting desolation. At that precise moment, Justine Henin was facing the world's media to explain one of the biggest upsets in Wimbledon history. 'I still don't understand what happened,' she admitted with alarming honesty.

This was meant to be her year. She had won everything else in tennis that was worth winning, absolutely everything. Now she was finally closing in on Wimbledon, the last jewel in her crown. Justine had beaten Serena Williams for the first time on grass in their quarter-final, and she was making Marion Bartoli look very ordinary in the semi-final. Henin, the top seed, the best in the world, had crushed Bartoli 6-1 in their first set on Centre Court. Her footwork, as superb as ever, helped her to maintain a hold on her clumsy opponent by breaking Bartoli in the very first game of the second set. Justine even served at 4-3. Two more games and it would have been over. Then Bartoli spotted Bond. James Bond. Pierce Brosnan was in the crowd, and it suddenly became clear to Marion that he was supporting her.

'When I saw James Bond cheering for me, I knew I couldn't let him down,' she said later. But she nearly did even then. Although she broke Justine back, the favourite went 0-30 ahead on Marion's serve at 5-5 in the second, and even squandered two break points. Somehow the killer instinct had deserted Henin, along with her customary sparkle, and a supercharged Bartoli moved into overdrive.

The underdog took that second set 7-5 and never looked back. With Brosnan smiling appreciatively, Marion played almost faultless tennis, full of power and confidence. She managed to take the first five games of the final set, even though Justine wasn't playing at all badly. It was one of the most amazing turnarounds Wimbledon had ever seen, and the crowd was loving it. But Thomas and Justine's new friend Greg Philippin – a good-looking young politician from Ans, near Liege, Belgium – weren't joining in the cheers. More likely they were struggling to understand what had gone wrong.

Somehow Henin avoided the dreaded 6-0 'doughnut', but all her renowned fighting spirit had disappeared. Bartoli won 1-6, 7-5, 6-1, and Justine's Wimbledon dream was over for another year. 'I don't think it was pressure,' reflected Justine in her post-match press conference. 'I lost a lot of energy in the last few weeks. Winning the French Open and the quarter-final against Serena was tiring emotionally. It was hard to be at my best.'

Her brother Thomas had been through too much in his

own life to feel distraught for very long about a tennis match. And right then he had too much to be happy about, despite his sister's defeat. The fact that he had been a companion to Justine during Wimbledon 2007, just as he had at Mons in the mid-1990s, was a remarkable and happy development for both of them. Justine and Thomas had once been so close, then they had disowned each other, and now it seemed they were almost as close as they had been before. Back in 2003, Thomas had appeared quite highly strung; a slim, pale, good-looking man, hiding behind a beard and working in a bank. Now he had put on weight but he was running his own bar and he seemed so much happier. Even in the rain after that shocking defeat, Thomas Henin put on a brave face without much effort, although the rate at which the rounds of drinks were arriving probably helped us hide the disappointment.

Greg, who had studied in the USA and returned to Belgium to carve out a successful career in politics, seemed philosophical about what had happened. He certainly wasn't knocking back the bottles of beer like we were. Here, you sensed, was someone level-headed enough to be good friends with Justine and Thomas, without coming between them, if indeed his involvement with the Henin family was to continue or deepen.

In the Belgian media later that summer, Thomas strenuously denied that Justine had ever been romantically involved with Greg, who also claimed they were 'just good friends'. Whatever the nature of Greg's relationship with Justine at the time of Wimbledon in 2007, and whatever direction her private life eventually took, you felt confident that she would ensure one thing: that her next serious boyfriend would make the greatest possible effort to get on with her family, even in the face of provocation, in order to avoid any fresh outbreak of war. Jose insisted: 'I don't think she'll ever choose anyone who would go against the family again.' Then, chuckling, he added. 'But I'll always agree to accept her next boyfriend if she agrees to accept my next girlfriend.'

In reality there was precious little romance in the air after that crushing Wimbledon semi-final defeat, only a defiant refusal to allow the hurt to show. It was only tennis after all. 'Win or lose we always booze' was our mindless motto that afternoon, as Thomas waited for Justine to complete her tournament obligations to the world's media. It was a hollow slogan, of course, but then again we were experiencing a pretty empty feeling in comparison to the one we had hoped for, the thrilling anticipation of a Wimbledon final. The electricity we all thought would be crackling in the air by this particular time in the afternoon had gone for us, replaced by damp.

Somewhere close by in the gloom, Carlos Rodriguez must have been working out how to prevent such a nasty surprise from ever happening again. For we suddenly spotted his son, Manuel, climbing the staircase which runs from an open floor of the players' hospitality area to the spectacular upper floor, with its views out across the Wimbledon courts and beyond. The problem was that young Manuel, who couldn't have been much more than six at the time, had elected to scale this open staircase on the outside of the safety rail. If he had lost his grip on the rail, he faced a dangerous fall.

I rushed across and persuaded the boy to jump down into my arms, which he agreed to do somewhat reluctantly. He probably did this sort of climb all the time, and his confidence was impressive enough to suggest that he had never fallen. He seemed to be wondering what the fuss was all about, and why someone was so determined to spoil his fun. Better safe than sorry, I thought, enough had gone wrong for one day. To make up for having played the villain, I kicked a football around with master Rodriguez on the grass-covered middle floor of the players' hospitality building. Manuel professed himself to be a David Beckham fan, and football helped us to forget the minor tennis disaster we had just witnessed.

In sporting terms, that late summer afternoon at Wimbledon was about as bleak as they come. 'It was a lesson in humility,' said Justine later, hinting perhaps that she had thought she had the match in the bag, and may already have been thinking of a probable final against her old rival – and the eventual champion – Venus Williams. It remained to be seen how many more chances for Wimbledon glory would come Justine's way. But Thomas and little Manuel showed that there were more important things in life, such as family and children. And besides, there would be other, much greater days yet to come in Justine's career. We didn't know it, but we wouldn't have long to wait.

Fast-forward a few more weeks, and Justine was setting Flushing Meadows alight. Poor Serena Williams was her victim at the quarter-final stage, 7-6, 6-1. The American became so angry when she realised that Henin would end her hopes yet again, that she was caught by the cameras apparently cursing her opponent. Video footage was released on the Internet soon afterwards, replaying the extraordinary moment again and again. The word that leaves Serena's mouth on that footage, as she prepares to receive and drills her opponent with a disdainful stare, is unmistakable. That word is: 'Bitch.'

She wasn't much more generous about Henin's victory in the post-match press conference, overcome perhaps at finding herself in a 'groundhog day' so soon after the quarter-final defeat at Wimbledon. 'She just made a lot of lucky shots and I made a lot of errors,' claimed Serena somewhat unsportingly. Losing to Justine in big matches was becoming a habit.

The difference at the US Open was that Henin had to face Serena's sister, Venus, in the semi-final. As Venus pointed out, the family honour of 'team Williams' was at stake, and it was fair to say that she intended to make the European girl pay for exposing her sister's limitations.

When battle commenced, it was Venus who won some of the most memorable points, finishing 16- and 27-stroke rallies with startling cross-court forehands. But Justine won the most important ones, including most of those in the first-set tie-break – and with outrageous audacity during the second set she even lobbed the six foot one inch Williams, a soul-destroying piece of improvisation which left Venus and her elegant frame looking considerably diminished. In sharp contrast Justine was dancing with joy inside, a child-like sensation that had seemed to her inconceivable not long before. One moment in particular stuck in her mind when the big screen caught her eye.

'I remember watching this replay of me winning a point,' she recalled. 'It was a drop-shot volley at one-love, deuce in the second set against Venus. It was an amazing shot, but the thing that struck me was the expression on my face, a look of passion and surprise. "Wow! How did you do that?" And it felt like I was a little girl enjoying her tennis again.'

They were fighting each other so hard and the level of tennis was so extraordinarily high that their bodies had to give eventually. Henin had trouble breathing in the second set, she had begun to suffer from asthma. Venus had to call the trainer because she was in even worse shape. 'I was feeling dizzy, a little sick to the stomach, having some energy problems,' she said afterwards. 'I'm not sure what's wrong with me.'

Justine had that effect on plenty of players in the early 21st century. And she exploited her weakening opponent to go 5-3 ahead – only to be broken back by a defiant Venus when no one expected more resistance. Williams finally ran out of steam in the 10th game, and missed a forehand when she needed accuracy to survive. The 7-6, 6-4 scoreline barely told the story of one of the most memorable clashes of wills in US Open history. 'I just went with my heart and kept fighting,' Justine said later. Her achievement was hard to exaggerate. Martina Hingis had beaten both Williams sisters in a Grand Slam, the Australian Open in 2001; but Justine had done it in their own back yard. Besides, Hingis had failed to go on and win that tournament in Melbourne, while Justine's Grand Slam chances in New York were still alive.

Waiting in the final was the familiar figure of Svetlana Kuznetsova, someone Justine had the happy habit of beating in big matches. Sure enough, she broke in the very first game, and repeated the feat to go 3-0. The thick-limbed Kuznetsova couldn't quite match Henin's mobility around the court; and the psychological block she seemed to have developed over a series of defeats to Justine meant she was fighting a losing battle. After one hour and 22 minutes, it was all over, 6-1, 6-3. As with the French Open,

Justine had taken a Grand Slam event without losing a set. It was a phenomenal display, from the surprising angles she found to undo her opponent, to the amazing array of shots that delighted the crowds. No one moved around a court quite like Justine Henin; no one's footwork was so quick that they could live with her, either in defence or attack. The fighting spirit was back, the strokeplay sublime; she had hit new heights and she was well aware that she was now very close to becoming the complete player.

Asked to place her seventh Grand Slam triumph in context, Justine said later: 'This was maybe the most important one. The quality I played in the last few matches is amazing. It's such a great feeling because I had a tough draw and I had a lot of things to prove to myself – not to anyone else, just to myself – and I did it.'

She once admitted that she used to be scared of the Williams sisters, but not any more. That fear was gone forever. And if she had wondered deep down whether she could thrive at the US Open without Pierre-Yves, she had just supplied the answer. Back in 2003 the young lovers had joked about the keys to his motorbike, they had laughed together in her moment of triumph, they had looked happier than ever. Now the marriage was gone, but the tennis of a US Open champion was still hers to summon at will. Henin wasn't just as good as she had been as Henin-Hardenne – she was even better.

It wasn't about standing alone, though, and she never pretended to be an island. 'The fact that I have my family back in my life helps a lot for sure,' she confirmed in her moment of victory. 'That gives me peace.'

CHAPTER 32
JUSTINE AND STEFFI – TENNIS SISTERS

SITTING THERE IN MANNHEIM, GERMANY, JUSTINE AND Steffi might almost have been sisters, such was their chemistry, mutual admiration and respect. The occasion in October 2007 was a series of exhibition tennis matches in Steffi Graf's home town, to raise money for her 'Children for Tomorrow' cancer charity. Goran Ivanisevic had played earlier, and young Ana Ivanovic too, proving that Croats and Serbs really can work together these days. Goran and Justine had played and beaten Steffi and her husband Andre Agassi at mixed doubles; then Agassi had almost lost to the much younger Ana in a stunning one-setter, which had turned a little too serious before Andre finally prevailed.

Steffi, of course, had loomed large in Justine's life even when she was very small, as she reminded us in Mannheim. 'I used to look at it and dream I would be like her. I was six or seven years old when I got into tennis like that.'

'That's how old I am!', Steffi interjected sadly, and everyone laughed.

Pausing to laugh herself, Justine continued: 'I found myself in the stand at Roland Garros in 1992 with my mother, and I was very sad when Steffi lost that French Open final to Monica Seles. But I told my mum that day: "One day I will be out there and I will be champion." Steffi was the person I most admired and respected then – and she still is.' Out on court Justine had taken the microphone and said: 'Steffi, you are one of the reasons why I'm playing tennis, you were important to me when I was a child.'

Steffi Graff was only too well aware of the tragedies that had dogged the life of the girl she inspired, and the passion they shared for alleviating the suffering of children with cancer, and the distress of their families. She knew that Justine had her own foundation for children with cancer – 'Justine's Winners Circle' – and that every July, whatever happened at Wimbledon, she'd spend 10 days at a camp with the children, to help them enjoy a normal holiday.

But July wasn't the only month in her busy year that Henin found time to think of those less fortunate than herself, far from it. Indeed, before 2007 was over, Justine would spend unpublicised hours at her own exhibition weekend in Charleroi, Belgium, being photographed with her arm around hundreds of thrilled kids, signing autographs and making everyone she met feel special, whatever their age. So when Steffi began to plan her November charity event in her home town, she knew Justine would respond positively if she could. As two great champions with big hearts, they already had a special connection.

Steffi told us: 'You know what, we've been getting to know each other over the last few years, and she was literally my first phone call.' Then Graf paid Justine an extraordinary tribute: 'What she has achieved in tennis and hopefully will in the future has been so remarkable. But what really stands out for me is her personality. Justine has a very quiet demeanour, and it hasn't been too easy for her in the last few years, and the way she has handled herself through everything . . .' Steffi suddenly became self-conscious. ' . . . It's hard to talk about her now she's sitting right here.'

'I'll move,' Justine joked. It brought the house down.

When the laughter had subsided, Steffi finished what she wanted to say. 'But she has handled everything with class and dedication to her sport and the people around her, that's what stands out.'

Agassi had saluted Justine at the end of the exhibition matches with the following tribute. 'Justine is one of the most talented women ever to have played the game of tennis.' Now, however, asked his opinion of her, Andre almost risked upsetting his wife by adding: 'If I could have hit my backhand like hers I would have taken it . . . I think if Steffi had had Justine's backhand she would even have been . . .' There was some nervous laughter; and at that moment Andre might have realised that perhaps he wasn't showing quite enough respect for his wife's astonishing career. At any rate, he appeared to modify what he was going to say and, looking at Steffi almost for forgiveness, he completed his sentence like this ' . . . it would have been a good shot to have, huh? They're both amazing.' The ever-alert Agassi had talked his way out of trouble just in time.

Even in the relaxed atmosphere of Mannheim, Henin was asked repeatedly about her failure to win Wimbledon, and the pressure that was building. And it was here, above all, that we saw Steffi acting just like a big sister to the world's number one.

'Again?' Graf asked the persistent questioner, slightly outraged. 'There should not be any pressure on her after all she has done.' Then Steffi looked sideways to Justine and said: 'I don't think there is any pressure, right?'

There was a moment's silence. Justine couldn't help but smile. 'No, no,' she said with a warm sense of irony, and burst out laughing. 'No pressure at all.' Once again the Mannheim comedian had stolen the show.

Then Graf came out with the line that would probably stay in Justine's mind the longest. She faced the media and insisted: 'If anyone can win Wimbledon so soon after winning Roland Garros in the modern era, Justine can. You need to trust her. And she needs to trust herself.'

Justine was slightly more serious now. 'I'll remember that,' she said to Steffi warmly, as if still looking up to her heroine. When the girl whose poster you had on your bedroom wall as a child tells you that you are good enough to do something, you had better believe it – no matter how many cynical old hacks are trying to write you off.

CHAPTER 33
THE MADRID MARATHON

THE TIMES OF LONDON CALLED IT 'ONE OF THE MOST dramatic tennis matches in history'. Even though newspapers sometimes tend to get carried away; the Sunday afternoon in November 2007, when Justine Henin played Maria Sharapova in the WTA Championships in Madrid, will linger long in the memory. And by the time they had finished knocking seven bells out of each other, that explosive afternoon had turned into a nail-biting evening.

No one in tennis had more fighting spirit than Henin and Sharapova. That was the one thing they had in common, because it was Maria who had the movie-star looks, the glamorous profile and greater commercial opportunities. Somehow Sharapova managed to stay totally dedicated to her tennis too, and that was to her credit. She had been world number one herself, an incredible achievement given the way her beauty had placed so many potential distractions in her path. For Justine, however, professional life had often appeared simpler.

Henin once said: 'Yes I like fashion and shopping but I don't have that much time to go to fashion shows. I'm a tennis player, and I'm really focused on my tennis, because it takes a lot of time to do fashion shoots . . . I would never rearrange my tennis practice to fit in with a photo shoot. It's important to me that I feel pretty but I'm very professional, I know why I'm here . . . I love being on court. I don't have the feeling that I was born to be famous, I was born to be a tennis player. When you look at some players you can talk about their results, and others more about what they're doing off the court, or what they're wearing – which I think is great, it's good for tennis.'

With Maria Sharapova you could talk about both, and Justine knew it. This particular day, however, would be remembered for tennis and nothing else; which was just as well because there was plenty at stake. If Justine won as expected, she would equal her good friend Steffi Graf's own personal record, a 25-match unbeaten run. Henin would also become the first woman to win 10 tour titles in a year since Martina Hingis a decade earlier. And she would become the first woman ever to earn $5 million in competition earnings in a single year. In short, Wimbledon or no Wimbledon, Henin's place among the all-time greats would be assured forever.

Sharapova had enjoyed a few weeks' rest while a shoulder injury healed, and her form in the WTA Championships had surprised many. If she beat Justine it meant she was back with a bang and ready to take her on again for that world number one crown in 2008. Henin's consistency had surprised no one; but by the time the final arrived she looked jaded. Indoor tennis, she always maintains, is tougher on the joints; the hard surface takes its toll, and a series of matches against the world's best at the end of a long season is the ultimate test of stamina and determination. She predicted: 'It's going to be a tough one, Maria has nothing to lose and she is back to her best.'

Justine wasn't wrong. Her own backhand misfired during the first set, and she was serving to stay in contention at 5-6. With a 49 per cent first serve success rate compared to Sharapova's punishing 83 per cent, Henin was up against it. Carlos Rodriguez sat open-mouthed as Henin double-faulted twice when it mattered, then failed to clear the net with an easy chance under no obvious pressure. Suddenly Sharapova had a deserved set point, although Justine saved it with a clubbing forehand. Soon a determined Maria earned herself a second set point, and this time she hit long to waste it. Henin couldn't put the game away either, and over-hit by a fraction to gift her opponent a third chance to claim the set. An aggressive drive-volley helped Justine to save that one too; but she ruined her good work with more poor judgement to present the glamour girl with set point number four. This time Maria was so wild and long in her execution that Rodriguez actually laughed out loud with relief.

Sharapova wiped the smile off the face of Justine's coach by setting up a fifth set point; and for once the Belgian girl came up with a big serve to ease the pressure. Henin was annoyed at being caged like this for so long, with deuce her only respite from Sharapova's assault. But when the world number one pushed a weak effort into the net, the entranced Madrid crowd braced themselves for set point number six. Typically, Justine found a bruising forehand just when she needed it, and we were back to deuce yet again. With enthralling imperfection, this repetitive dance continued.

There were gasps of disbelief when Justine blundered her way to a fourth double-fault in this extraordinary 12th game alone, and it looked as though her ball-toss was way too low for comfort. Surely Sharapova couldn't squander a seventh set point? A deep, booming backhand from Justine gave us the answer, and she screamed 'Allez' in triumph. This was a stubborn streak bordering on the ridiculous, and when Henin conjured a big serve on the next point she was on the verge of forcing the tie-break. Inexplicably she volleyed into the net, and wasted another chance to close out soon afterwards.

Was this amazing game ever going to end? Justine's trademark backhand down the line drifted carelessly wide and Sharapova had her eighth set point. You had to admire Maria's persistence, and the forgiveness she managed to show herself for her own lack of ruthlessness. Many lesser players would have imploded by now, and beaten them-selves up for wasting all those opportunities over the previous 15 minutes or more. Instead she turned the screw one more time, and Justine completely mis-hit a desperate return. It cost Henin the set, and in a rare show of temperament she threw her racket on the floor. Sharapova, howling in triumph, had ended one of the biggest set-point sagas in memory.

Justine should have hit straight back in the first game of the second set, before her opponent had regained her composure, but she squandered three break points of her own. Maria hit an ace at 116mph to underline her overall superiority in that department, and went 2-1 ahead. On they went, putting more and more weight behind their shots and refusing to give an inch. Finally, a big Justine return saw Sharapova scrambling into oblivion, and the favourite had a break to go 5-4 ahead. Shooting herself in the foot with remarkable accuracy, Henin came up with an unforced error in the very next game and gave Maria break-back at 5-5.

It wasn't necessarily the all-round quality of the tennis that made this match unforgettable, it was the sheer sense of theatre generated. Minutes later Sharapova challenged an out call that had signalled break point. The replay supported the original verdict. Henin blew her chance with a mis-hit and Carlos looked dejected. He soon cheered up when Justine blasted a backhand straight at the server, who had no answer. But Henin wasted the second break point too, only to forgive herself and fashion a third. Carlos clapped urgently, summoning Henin's killer instinct. The way the match had gone so far, he couldn't have been too confident of receiving the response he was hoping for.

Sharapova, who had looked her usual gorgeous self at the start of proceedings, now looked tired, pale, sweaty and spotty. She hit too long when it really mattered, and Henin was serving for the set again at 6-5. This wasn't likely to be as straightforward as it looked either, so the Madrid crowd and the millions watching on TV took a deep breath and prepared to witness another marathon game. However, blink and you would have missed it. Three mistakes by Maria, three set points, a scorching Henin forehand and it was over. Justine shook her fist and another shrill 'Allez' told the story. After all that huffing and puffing, each woman had taken a set 7-5 and you couldn't separate them.

There were signs, however, that Sharapova was feeling the pace more than Justine. She disappeared for an interminable toilet break, as if trying to buy herself some recovery time; after those epic first two sets no one could blame her. But she couldn't disguise the fatigue, and she began to double-fault as often as Justine had done earlier. They almost slugged themselves to a standstill on one break point. Henin won the war of attrition, and consolidated on serve to go 3-1 ahead.

An increasingly desperate Maria dug out an ace and fired some more big shells to find a foothold at 2-3. At the changeover she took the opportunity to call for the trainer. 'I can't even swallow sometimes,' she complained, pointing to her throat. She spluttered on her drink, and a doctor was looking at her closely. There had been no visible signs of distress before, other than the general physical exhaustion that playing Justine Henin often caused her opponents. Maria accepted a nose spray to clear her tubes and went back to work, having earned herself another important breather. It paid off too, because she conjured a truly breathtaking cross-court forehand to set up a break-back point. Henin had no answer and they were level again at 3-3.

The seventh game of that final set brought one of the shots of the match. A Sharapova lob sent Justine back-pedalling. That motion, combined with her lack of height and inevitable fatigue, all seemed to be working against her. But under such pressure Henin came up with a sumptuous deep smash that was completely unanswerable. She followed up during the next point with a superb defensive forehand, and a stunned Maria got her angles all wrong. Suddenly Justine had three break points; and although she wasted one of them, Sharapova crumbled into a double-fault to put her rival in the driving seat.

Sharapova called for the trainer again, and Justine looked lost in thought, her mouth covered by her towel. When they got up to play again, Henin produced her finest game. A big serve gave her the perfect start. But the next point looked lost until Justine conjured an impossibly brilliant defensive backhand, leaving an unprepared Maria to drive her volley into the net. Henin's next serve was only 81mph, but the wide angle was the key. Finally Justine wore down her opponent in a long and draining rally, and it was 5-3.

Sharapova's aim was deserting her, and it was soon championship point to the world's greatest at 30-40. Carlos urged his player on, the crowd applauded in keen anticipation of a kill . . . and Maria saved the match with an all-or-nothing forehand that landed right on the line. You had to admire her courage, and it was easy to see why she too had been a world number one in the recent past. After four deuces, however, she double-faulted again, and Henin had her second opportunity to close out a thriller. To add to the drama, Justine seemed to slip slightly and her shot didn't make it over the net.

Teetering on the brink, Maria misjudged another one and gifted her opponent a third championship point. Prolonging the tension, Henin misjudged the spin and returned serve into the net. But Carlos didn't want any more stress, it had been a long season. And when Sharapova hit wide at the end of a long rally to hand Justine yet another match point, Rodriguez was out of his seat. 'Allez JuJu' he shouted, 'Come on JuJu.'

Unfortunately for Rodriguez and his peace of mind, however, there was nothing his player could do when Maria served straight down the middle to force yet another deuce. Surely someone had to back down eventually? Sharapova's nerves looked shredded when she lashed out wildly to expose herself to an extraordinary fifth championship point of the game. Justine needed to produce only one more piece of class and the title was hers. She found a big forehand, Maria for once just couldn't reply, and Justine, as she had done so many times over the years, threw her racket away in relief and joy. Three hours and 24 minutes had passed since they had started, the longest match the WTA Championships had known.

Arms outstretched, as if to illustrate her ordeal, Justine milked the applause of an audience almost as drained emotionally as she was. Then she climbed some steps and dashed along the rows of seats past astonished spectators, falling into the arms of new members of her entourage and Carlos too.

Back on court she admitted: 'That was a tough last game, we were both dead. The third set was mental and physical and I knew I could handle the pressure.' Sharapova had already paid tribute to her conqueror. 'She's had an incredible, incredible year. She's gone through so much in her life, she is someone who has succeeded, on and off the court. It is an honour to play against her.'

Even Bjorn Borg, one of the greatest tennis legends of them all, had hailed Henin in glowing terms at around this time. Borg said: 'Justine is number one in the world, there is no debate about that. And if she stays free from injury, there is no reason why she cannot remain the women's number one for a long time to come.'

Such respect from one of the greats gave plenty of food for thought. But perhaps Sharapova's tribute was even more revealing, because it showed that her peers saw Justine as more than a tennis player. To be the best in the world at tennis, a sport so intensely gladiatorial, dangerously stressful and wonderfully dramatic, was already an extraordinary thing. But her rivals saw her as a symbol of triumph over tragedy, strength against the odds, and supreme dedication to her craft.

'Three hours and 24 minutes, can you believe it?' It was Alphonse Henin, now in his late 80s, still going strong having fought off his various ailments. I put in the call a few weeks after the Madrid marathon, to see what Alphonse and his wife Jeanne were making of the great family reconciliation. But the epic confrontation with Sharapova was still a natural focal point for both of us. For one thing that would never change, while he still lived and breathed, was the determination of Justine's grandfather to put himself through the agonies of her most dramatic matches by watching her from home. Even by his standards, however, this one had proved something of a trial. 'I've never had to watch Justine for that long in my life before,' he chuckled. 'Never!'

Here was a man who had almost died watching her 2001 French Open semi-final against Kim Clijsters, who had been through the heartbreak of the feud, exclusion from Justine's wedding, and much more. But what had he been doing on that particular Sunday afternoon in November 2007? Draining himself further in front of another cliff-hanger, which had of course been beamed live to his Belgian village above the caves of Han-sur-Lesse.

'Those double-faults she kept making. It was so hard,' he recalled.

I couldn't believe he had managed to watch the entire match without feeling sick with tension, or even suffering another stroke.

'Oh but I saw it all, every minute,' he insisted. 'I have to support her. She is my granddaughter. And besides, she has made the effort to come and see us four or five times recently, very thoughtful considering how busy she has been. Of course, Justine has changed in some ways during the time she has been away, but she's still a nice girl.' Alphonse and Jeanne, joint heads of the Henin family, had always said they would leave their door open. And finally Justine had walked back in; and in that moment her grandparents had received their reward for never giving up hope.

'Three hours and 24 minutes,' repeated Alphonse, shortly before we wished each other well and said goodbye. 'You think Justine looked tired at the end? You should have seen me!'

The historic match and its result had provided a comfort of sorts, given what had been going on behind the scenes. Alphonse and I both knew that the backdrop to this win had been far more important, although I didn't want to upset the old man by talking about a subject that was still so hard for everyone to take in.

CHAPTER 34
A LIFE TOO SHORT

TWO DAYS AFTER SHE WON THE MADRID MARATHON, Justine Henin attended the funeral of her sister Sarah's baby son, Romain.

During November, the tennis star had somehow found the concentration, professionalism and even the humour to fulfil her public obligations. In private she had faced indescribable anguish, and cried countless times over the sheer helplessness of her situation. Whether sitting alongside her heroine Steffi Graf in Mannheim, or lifting the WTA trophy in Spain, there was somewhere else Justine Henin would rather have been – by her sister Sarah's side as she went through every woman's worst nightmare.

I had been with their brother David, in his 'Saint Paul Gourmand' restaurant in Liege, when we realised that an event which should have been one of the happiest in the Henin family's troubled history was about to turn to tragedy. David had just been reminding me of the joyful arrival they were already keenly anticipating as a family. 'In five months' time my sister Sarah will become a mother,' he beamed.

'No one deserves that more than Sarah,' I replied. 'She has had to put up with so much, and she has stayed positive all the way through, she is such a great person.' Literally five minutes after we exchanged those words, David received a call from Jose. Sarah had just been for her baby's 20-week scan, that nerve-racking, defining moment for most modern-day parents in the developed world. We all pray the scan will show up no abnormalities in our baby, we all fear it might. Most people leave hospital laughing with relief, excited for the future. For a small minority, however, that scan signals the start of a terrible ordeal, during which some tough, often heartbreaking decisions have to be made. Sarah was among the unfortunate minority. Her baby's heart was defective, and there were other complications. In short, there was no hope of the unborn child surviving.

David broke the news to me; and even for an outsider, who had simply grown fond of the family over the years, it was a tough blow to take. For the family members themselves, it must have been devastating, particularly after all they had been through.

Jose called me a few minutes later. He was distraught, and his tears were infectious. 'How much more do we have to take?' he cried. 'Poor Sarah. I was so happy for her.' David kept his emotions more firmly under control, though he muttered something along the lines of: 'It always happens to us.'

It was hard to know what to say, it always is in such circumstances. Many families go through one or more of the tragedies that have befallen the Henins; but all of those personal setbacks, raining down on one little group of people? It had been cruel beyond belief. The Henin family, resilient as the survivors are, would probably argue that they have also enjoyed several blessings. Many of their children have grown up to become happy, healthy adults, and one had even become a world champion in her field. But for other Henin children, life was far too short. And familiarity with that type of tragedy would never make it any easier to bear.

Justine was stranded in Germany, preparing for Steffi Graf's charity event, when she heard the dreadful news. Stunned, she rang her distraught sister to offer what support she could from afar. But when she spoke to her father, her own sorrow overwhelmed her, and she cried bitter tears at not being able to comfort Sarah in person in her hour of need. 'First she felt terrible for Sarah,' explained Jose. 'Then she felt guilty because she wasn't there; and she was openly asking herself why it was that whenever something horrible like this happened, she was always somewhere else. I think for her it brought back memories of when Thomas lost his baby, and she was over in the United States.'

Graf's exhibition matches in Mannheim were for children with cancer, and Henin couldn't just pack up and leave. Those who might think the life of a sports star is easy should consider a little what Justine had to go through in Germany that day. Essentially, she was part of a star act for charity, with Andre Agassi, Goran Ivanisevic, Steffi Graf and Ana Ivanovic her co-stars. She had to play to the crowd, laugh along with the slapstick routines invented by the others, and even crack jokes in a combined press conference when the matches were over. She had to push her immense sadness over her sister's plight into some dimly lit corner of her inner being, while she played

'Justine Henin, tennis star'. How awful to be in a situation where you have to smile and smile when all the time you are bursting with grief and worry. It is quite possible that, among all the boisterous thousands in the packed German arena, only Justine, her small entourage and I knew what she was going through, and how bravely she was fulfilling her obligations to Steffi and her cancer charity. Like most clichés, the one about it being lonely at the top is there for a reason.

Meanwhile we all prayed for a miracle, that subsequent tests would prove more optimistic for Sarah's baby, that maybe she had been the victim of some cruel medical misjudgement in the first instance.

When the tennis show was over, Justine rushed from Mannheim to Liege to be at her sister's side. At least she would have been of some comfort when the brutal confirmation of Sarah's predicament came through. And if Justine had shown such strength in Mannheim, you can be sure she showed even more as she provided a shoulder for Sarah to cry on in her darkest moments.

But for all her compassion, Justine couldn't change anything, and her tennis schedule soon pulled her away from her family again. Her sister continued to wrestle with a heartbreaking dilemma, surrounded by others who loved her. Soon it became clear what would have to be done, although that clarity made the procedure no easier to contemplate. Sadly, bravely, inevitably, Sarah Henin and her supportive partner Louis decided that it was best for everyone's sake to induce the baby early and bring an end to the misery. The only alternative would have been that same misery, drawn out over an even more agonising period of time.

By the time the doctors were ready, Justine had left for Madrid and the Masters tournament. She knew that Sarah would be supported by others who loved her just as much, and the sisters could talk by phone, although it would have been no easier for the tennis star to concentrate on work at such a terrible time.

Baby Romain's soul left this earth all too soon, and it would be futile for anyone on the outside even to pretend to understand the pain of a mother and father involved in such a tragedy. Sometimes such bleak moments can be made even more excruciating for the grieving parents by the failure of others to understand that even the shortest life is still a life, and that the baby is an individual whose passing should be respected like the death of any other human being. There was no such mistake within the Henin family, and there was never any doubt that the funeral would be attended by all those the bereaved couple, Louis and Sarah, wanted to be there.

Justine, who, as a teenager, had missed the funeral of Thomas' six-week-old son Emilien, wasn't about to make the same mistake twice. The official farewell to Romain would take place just after the WTA final in Madrid, and nothing was going to stop the tennis star from joining the other mourners. The only question was whether the world number one was going to play in Spain that week at all. Jose revealed: 'That's why Justine was so anxious at the start of the Masters in Madrid. The public didn't know what she was feeling because she is strong; but she is sensitive too, and some of the Belgian journalists who know her quite well saw that something was wrong. They told her: "You look so strange, so different. Has something happened?" And of course she couldn't explain anything.'

A big part of Justine didn't want to be in the spotlight at all at such a desolate moment, and she discussed her predicament with her father. Jose told her this: 'You're in Madrid so play if you feel you can. Even though it's difficult for you, please play your matches as you had planned to do before this happened, and do your best because that would be nice for Sarah too.'

We already know how she responded, about the memorable climax to the tournament, which might seem even more astonishing given the highly emotional background. 'She did her maximum for Sarah,' Jose said later. 'She played her best tennis for her little sister. When she won against Sharapova, in such difficult psychological conditions, it gave Sarah something, just the smallest consolation, which is all it could ever be after what had happened to her. But it was something.' And at least Sarah was spared the added anguish that would have come with knowing her own tragic circumstances had derailed her sister's season, something that might easily have happened, given Justine's turmoil at the start of the week.

Henin the tennis star had her moment of glory in Madrid, but she was even happier to get away. 'The next day she was back with us,' revealed Jose later, 'ready to go to the cemetery with the rest of us for the funeral.'

She may have earned $5 million on the tennis circuit in 2007, but no one who had inside knowledge of the torment she was going through during those terrible November weeks will have envied her celebrity. When you are aware of a famous person's private hell, and you see them having to perform on the public stage in order to fulfil so many people's expectations, you start to think they might just be worth every dime they earn.

It is no wonder that so many celebrities become casualties during their high-pressure careers, falling victim to various tempting addictions. Somehow Justine has come to terms with the cauldron in which she conducts her professional life. Her only addiction, self-confessed, is to tennis. But these days her love for her family matches and perhaps even surpasses her love for her sport. So the pain she felt and witnessed that month made her think more deeply about what her father had been through when he lost his own infant.

Jose confided: 'One day Justine came to me and she said: "After Sarah lost her baby I understand much better the impact that losing Florence had on you, and how it made you protective and over-anxious around me. I know you much better now, Papa."'

CHAPTER 35
LOVE ALL

ON 15 DECEMBER, 2007, SOMETHING QUITE EXTRA-ordinary happened, a miracle which would have seemed impossible a year earlier: Jose Henin watched his daughter play a tennis match. It didn't sound like much, but for this family it was the equivalent of the Berlin Wall coming down, or Man's first walk on the moon.

Six thousand people came to watch the Sixth Women's Tennis Trophy, played in an indoor arena called the Spiroudome in Charleroi, Belgium. One person meant more than most to Justine that day, and he was first to arrive.

As she warmed up, a couple of hours before the doors to the tournament officially opened, Jose was already courtside, savouring the moment for which he had waited so long. When Justine had finished her pre-match loosen-ing routine, she strolled over. 'Hi Papa,' she chirped casually, as though it were the most natural thing in the world for the father she had disowned for seven years to be with her at such a moment.

I was there too, along with a Paris-based photographer called Paul Cooper, and we were hoping that Justine would agree to pose for a picture with her 'Papa' out on the tennis court itself. Jose explained the situation to Justine, and surprisingly she agreed without so much as a moment's hesitation. 'You're very lucky,' Jose told us. 'This is the first time we've been out on a tennis court together since 2000, and the first picture we've had taken together at her place of work.'

They embraced for the camera, both grinning from ear to ear, the tennis star more than happy to acknowledge the reunion publicly. As they went up to the net, arm in arm, I couldn't help but think back to the last time I had seen them together, at the Han-sur-Lesse tennis club back in 2001. With Pierre-Yves Hardenne prowling and scowling in the background, it had been their final conversation together for many painful years, and in essence the feud had already begun by then. Now, at last, all that was behind them, and would remain so for as long as they continued to respect each other, and remembered what very different individuals they were.

When the photo-shoot was over, I thanked Justine for her help and she smiled. She seemed to hold no grudges for past criticism. As she left the stage, albeit temporarily, those in the Charleroi Spiroudome who had witnessed darker days sat in silence, marvelling at the metamorphosis. 'She's relaxed, I'm relaxed, it's a dream,' her father said after a while. 'This is only an exhibition, but it's an important step for us.'

What made the wait for Justine's return all the more comfortable was that another important step had been taken a few weeks earlier, when peace had broken out between Justine's father and her coach, Carlos Rodriguez. The pair had propped up the bar in a television company's

VIP lounge in Monaco, where a programme was being made about the tennis star. No one would ever have thought they had been opposed to each other for the previous seven years, and no apologies had been considered necessary on either side.

Jose had described the breakthrough to me by phone a couple of days after the meeting. He said: 'We stayed a long time at the bar and we talked about Justine. We think exactly the same things about her.' Sensing my disbelief, he insisted: 'It's true. Carlos and me, friends together like before, why not? We just want to be positive for Justine. It is important to bear in mind that he didn't put up the slightest resistance to Justine coming back to her family, in fact he encouraged it.'

Suddenly the scene was reminiscent of the day Carlos and Jose had first met, when Justine had been a hungry 14-year-old, looking to improve. Eleven years later, Jose proclaimed: 'Carlos is right about the way to go for a better Justine. More and more positive, stronger in the head, going to the net, more volleys. He has already done a fantastic job for her and I can't ask for any more.'

Except, of course, to witness the 25-year-old Justine in action for himself. Jose waited patiently, and the knowledge that Carlos was in close proximity did nothing to spoil the precious sense of anticipation. Less than two hours later, Jose's latest dream became reality. He had taken his seat alongside his son, Thomas, and his daughter Sarah, in a section near one of the baselines. The lights were dimmed and the show began, as dancing lasers beamed Justine's profile onto the court. Dressed in bright blue, she made a big entrance to the booming sound of the Tina Turner classic, 'Simply the Best'. The other players, Nadia Petrova,

Anna Chakvetadze and Francesca Schiavone couldn't argue with the theme tune.

The crowd went crazy as Justine's triumphant year was played back on video, and one statistic stood out. To win 63 matches out of 67 takes some doing in any sport. Now, with year-end fatigue setting in, she wanted to win just one more time – for her father. Petrova was her powerful opponent; and after Justine took the first set 6-4, the tall Russian threatened to spoil the party by taking the second 6-1, but Henin wiped away a 0-2 deficit in the final set to go 3-2 ahead. The arena broke into a Mexican wave to celebrate a trademark comeback, Jose joined in, and so did a smiling Justine on court. Times really had changed.

But it was the business end of the match, and it was time to get serious. Nadia drove long, an overweight baseline judge threw out an arm to call the ball out, and his chair gave way. Had it collapsed completely, he might have rolled away from the scene of his mishap and regained some composure almost before anyone had noticed. But the chair drew him down into its own distortion and left him there, sunken and lopsided, trapped in a moment of pure slapstick comedy that brought the house down. Had the baseline judge laughed at the absurdity of his situation, and played to the crowd, it would have been less funny. What brought tears to the eyes was his attempt to retain an air of authority. The big belly busting out of his skin-tight T-shirt, the moustache and glasses looking like a disguise from a joke shop, the baseball cap on a middle-aged head, all contributed to the glory of the moment.

Justine wasn't slow to notice. She walked over and asked the baseline judge if he was OK. 'Are you sure, you're not hurt?' When he replied that he was fine, she looked him over and said: 'Diet for you.'

Even Justine's sister, Sarah, almost fell off her chair laughing. It was good to see her swept away momentarily by the sheer joy of life, when so many recent days had seen her struggle to cope with her grief. In that moment you knew she would be OK. Jose was crying with laughter, and Thomas too. As someone replaced the offending chair, we thought we saw just the tiniest hint of a smile on the baseline judge's face, but we weren't sure.

Justine closed out the final set 6-4. Some of us believed that Petrova could have won the match if she had put her mind to it. But it would have been the most outrageous piece of party-pooping tennis had ever seen.

Justine took the microphone. 'Tonight was very special because it was the first time I had my father watching me from the stands,' she told the crowd. They stood and applauded, familiar with the story. You couldn't make it up. I realised as much the next day, when we all returned to the Spiroudome to watch Justine play Chakvetadze in the Women's Tennis Cup Final. I bumped into that unforgettable baseline judge and asked him what his name was. 'Henin,' he replied. This was getting silly. 'No, really,' he said, showing me his official tournament identification. 'Emile Henin. No relation, but we used to play at the same tennis club, Geronsart, when she was a tiny kid. We have known each other for ages.'

So that's why she had felt free to make her rather cheeky remark the previous night. I asked Emile whether he had minded so many people laughing at him. 'Not really,' he said sportingly. 'I saw Justine this morning. She came up to me and said: "I was supposed to be the star of this show and now it's you."'

Just before Justine played Anna, I saw her sister, Sarah. She was reading a newspaper with Jose, and they had printed a photograph of what Justine would look like in 40 years' time. 'It's my mother, Jeanne,' said Jose. 'It's the spitting image of Jeanne.' It was true. Sarah put away the paper so we could talk briefly; I asked her if she was alright, and she said she was. We didn't need to say any more, I'd written to her at the time of the tragedy, and words were useless anyway. It was time to lighten the mood.

'That poor baseline judge last night,' I said. Sarah grinned. 'And the funniest thing was that he just had the face for it.' Sarah was giggling again, and looking forward to Christmas. She and her partner Louis were to play host to the Henin family in their new house. 'We don't know what we're having yet, Louis has to shoot it first,' joked Jose. 'But Papa will be doing the cooking.'

Then I asked the most stupid question of all. 'Will it be nice to have Justine there, Sarah?' A deeper smile broke out on her face. 'Very,' she said. The true star of the Henin family never had been the type to use 10 words where one would do.

The final against Chakvetadze represented another landmark. David Henin had joined Jose, Thomas and Sarah in the crowd. It was the first time that Justine's entire, surviving immediate family had been reunited to watch her play live. To say that the Henin family deserved this happy moment would be an understatement. Three of the four spectators in question had suffered arguably the worst blow life can deliver, the loss of a first-born; the other had nearly died in a car crash. And yet there they all were, sitting in a row, together at last to cheer the girl they had never stopped loving.

Thomas bounced his second child, the eight-month-old Kiara, on his knee for most of the match, and Sarah played with the baby too; a defiant, poignant symbol, if ever there was one, of the fact that life goes on. And for the record Kiara was perfectly behaved, never once screaming a complaint about a line call on behalf of her aunt.

The thought of Justine losing this match was simply unthinkable, and she dispatched her compliant opponent 6-4, 6-2. Jose stood to applaud, his hands over his head, and Justine waved in her father's direction. He remained standing to film the victory ceremony, as local dignitaries presented the heroine with a handsome glass trophy. She had won two Grand Slams, the WTA Champtionships and seven other titles that year; but Jose was behaving like a proud father whose daughter had just won her first tournament at the local tennis club. It was touching to watch.

Later a television interviewer asked Justine about her Papa's enthusiasm. 'That's nice,' she said. 'It was really emotional because this weekend was the first time, for such a long time, that he was there. I think he was relieved that I actually won my two matches though,' she said. 'And my little goddaughter [Kiara] was so calm and beautifully behaved up there. It was very nice to have my family with me, it is marvellous to feel reunited as a group. This gives me a lot of courage for whatever comes next.'

By the end of 2007 Justine had won the International Tennis Federation World Championship and the USSA Athlete of the Year. She would win her 40th title in Sydney at the start of 2008, defeating world number three, Ana Ivanovic, in the semis and number two, Svetlana Kuznetsova, in the final after overcoming a 0-3 deficit in the third set. The unbeaten run would stretch to 32 matches, before a scintillating Maria Sharapova finally defeated Justine in the Australian Open quarter-final. Jose didn't join her on the trip Down Under, though he was looking forward to the European season.

'I'll go and see her sometimes, though not all the time,' admitted Jose. And he was in Antwerp, Belgium, along with 16,600 others, to watch his daughter claim her 41st tour title with a 6-3, 6-3 victory over Karin Knapp in February. A few days later Justine was crowned queen of the sporting Oscars when she was voted Laureus Sportswoman of the Year, 2008, at a glittering ceremony in St Petersburg, Russia. Her father was understandably proud of these achievements, and Jose couldn't hide his desire to be there if ever Justine completed her set of Grand Slams. He confessed, 'But Wimbledon is the biggest dream. I might have to put on a wig, false nose and beard, so she doesn't know I'm there on Centre Court. She'll win it or she won't, destiny will decide.' Then, looking me in the eye, he added. 'And if she does win it one day, let's swig champagne straight from the bottle, one each!'

He had a deal.